SOUTHEND UNITED

FOOTBALL CLUB

Classics

SOUTHEND UNITED
FOOTBALL CLUB

PETER MILES & DAVID GOODY

TEMPUS

*This book is dedicated to the late Jim Goody, a lifelong
Southend United supporter.*

Front cover illustration: Leon Cort (with grateful thanks to the *Evening Echo*).

First published 2005

Tempus Publishing Limited
The Mill, Brimscombe Port,
Stroud, Gloucestershire, GL5 2QG
www.tempus-publishing.com

British Library Cataloguing in Publication Data.
A catalogue record for this book is available from the British Library.

ISBN 0 7524 3072 6

Typesetting and origination by Tempus Publishing Limited
Printed and bound in Great Britain

Acknowledgements

We would like to acknowledge the continued co-operation of Southend United Football Club. Thanks go to the *Evening Echo* for the use of some of the pictures in this volume; and remember for news of the Blues read the *Evening Echo*. There are also grateful thanks to Phil Cox and Keith Roe for some additional material used in this volume. There is also much credit due to James Howarth and his staff at Tempus Publishing for their continuing efforts in promoting the profile of lesser clubs such as Southend United.

Every effort has been made to ensure that copyright has not been infringed, and apologies are offered should any such infringements have inadvertently occurred.

About the Authors

Peter Miles was born in London in 1969 and watched his first game at Roots Hall in 1976. He remains a regular at home and away games and lives close to the stadium. This is his fourth book on Southend United, all of which have been co-written with Dave Goody, and his eighth published football work. He is married to Cathy.

Dave Goody has one of the largest known collections of Southend United memorabilia, which has been amassed over a considerable period of time. Over a ten-year period he researched the statistics that formed the backbone of Peter Mason's 1993 club history. He lives in Hockley with his wife Karen and young sons Matthew and Samuel.

Introduction

There is nothing quite like going to a match that perhaps from the outset looks nothing more than 'just another game' but at the end of the ninety minutes leaves you fulfilled and excited. These matches can take many forms: great comebacks, crushing victories, triumphs over adversity and just plain old thrilling football matches. We have carefully chosen our selection to cover the breadth of the club's near-100-year history. We hope the fifty games chosen will revive some happy memories and recall just some of the great players that have represented Southend United.

This is our third book for Tempus Publishing, who publish many varied and interesting titles on football clubs, and we trust you will enjoy recalling some memorable matches that have punctuated the long history of our club.

Classic Matches

Union Berlin 0	Southend United 4	05/05/1910
Chelsea 5	Southend United 2	11/01/1913
Southend United 2	Brighton & Hove Albion 0	28/08/1920
Southend United 4	Derby County 1	30/01/1926
Clapton Orient 3	Southend United 1	06/12/1930
Southend United 10	Golders Green 1	24/11/1934
Tottenham Hotspur 4	Southend United 4	11/01/1936
Ipswich Town 4	Southend United 2	27/08/1938
Southend United 4	Chesterfield 3	16/01/1939
Bristol Rovers 1	Southend United 3	05/10/1946
Barnet 2	Southend United 9	14/12/1946
Southend United 8	Swindon Town 2	24/02/1951
Everton 3	Southend United 1	08/01/1955
Southend United 3	Norwich City 1	20/08/1955
Colchester United 3	Southend United 6	27/08/1955
Southend United 0	Manchester City 1	28/01/1956
Southend United 2	Liverpool 1	05/01/1957
Southend United 6	Queens Park Rangers 0	31/08/1957
Queens Park Rangers 4	Southend United 5	11/01/1964
Brighton & Hove Albion 9	Southend United 1	27/11/1965
Southend United 9	King's Lynn 0	16/11/1968
Southend United 10	Brentwood Town 1	07/12/1968
Tour to Russia		Summer 1971

Southend United 1	Cambridge United 2	21/04/1972
Walsall 2	Southend United 3	06/09/1975
Southend United 0	Liverpool 0	10/01/1979
Bolton Wanderers 1	Southend United 2	28/08/1979
Burnley 3	Southend United 5	20/04/1982
Scunthorpe United 1	Southend United 6	30/09/1983
Southend United 1	Torquay United 0	11/05/1985
Stockport County 0	Southend United 2	08/05/1987
Southend United 1	Derby County 0	22/09/1987
Aldershot 0	Southend United 5	09/09/1989
Southend United 3	Tottenham Hotspur 2	04/10/1989
Peterborough United 1	Southend United 2	05/05/1990
Southend United 10	Aldershot 1	06/11/1990
Southend United 7	Torquay United 0	26/02/1991
Bury 0	Southend United 1	04/05/1991
Southend United 1	Charlton Athletic 1	26/10/1991
Southend United 4	Newcastle United 0	01/01/1992
Southend United 3	Notts County 1	21/11/1992
Southend United 1	West Ham United 0	07/04/1993
Millwall 1	Southend United 4	22/08/1993
A.C. Fiorentina 3	Southend United 0	12/10/1993
Southend United 3	Birmingham City 1	01/01/1994
Charlton Athletic 4	Southend United 3	02/04/1994
Southend United 5	Bolton Wanderers 2	07/09/1996
Plymouth Argyle 3	Southend United 3	24/04/2001
Southend United 4	Rushden & Diamonds 2	26/12/2001
Southend United 4	Queens Park Rangers 0	20/01/2004

Union Berlin v. Southend United

5 May 1910   Friendly

An historic match and one of six matches played by Southend United in Germany, the club's first matches on foreign soil. The highly successful tour saw five wins with only one defeat, coming against Hertha Berlin. The tour closed with a 10-0 defeat of Oxford City, the first match between two English sides in Germany.

The match got underway in front of a disappointing crowd of 750, many spectators staying away due to the inclement weather that saw a tremendous downpour just prior to kick-off. Southend attacked from the off after Weisener had been dispossessed from the kick-off. Tom Murray burst forward and Union's half-back Buchmann handled his shot in the area. The referee, an Englishman by the name of Dutton, had no alternative but to award a penalty kick. Alex 'Nutty' King stepped up to take it but succeeded in shooting straight at the German goalkeeper, Paul Eichelmann. Luckily for King, Eichelmann's parry bounced back to his feet and he was able to stroke the ball into an unguarded net to give the Shrimpers a first-minute lead. Eichelmann was a small but extremely brave goalkeeper who would be selected for Germany on two occasions and had played some matches in England. Indeed, he had turned down contract offers from several English clubs.

Southend continued to attack and George Harrod shot narrowly wide from the game's first corner kick. Union's first attack ended with Zeidler hitting the side netting without troubling Southend's custodian, Percy Toone. Southend went 2-0 up after ten minutes when Harrod received a throw-in on the right from Murray. He took on the Berlin defence, which failed to offer an effective challenge. Harrod blasted the ball towards Eichelmann who was unable to stop the ball hitting the back of the net. The goal was met by polite applause from the locals, impressed by the ferocity of Harrod's shot. After an initial uncertain start, Eichelmann then saved his side from a total rout by stopping chance after chance, although Sutherland, King and Harrod were somewhat profligate in front of goal.

Union's best chance came after twenty-four minutes when Piscara crossed to Weisener and his shot bought a fine save from Toone. Toone then drew gasps from the crowd when his prodigious throw, past the halfway line, sent Louis Parke through for another attack. Alfred Frost was playing well in the middle of the field and one of his passes sent Billy Sutherland through, but Eichelmann managed to stop the ball before it crossed the line. Southend were dominant and Eichelmann produced a stunning save to thwart Harrod on the half-hour mark. Two minutes later the constant pressure saw Jurga handle a shot from King. This time Frost took the penalty but blasted wide of the target. Just before half-time King latched on to a through ball from Frost and gave Southend a 3-0 interval lead.

Although Union played better after the break, Frost, Sutherland and Harrod squandered further chances to increase the lead. The Germans then enjoyed a spell of pressure and were desperate to

---

UNION BERLIN 0   **SOUTHEND UNITED 4**

King (3), Harrod

Above left: Alex King scored an excellent hat-trick for the tourists.

Above right: George Harrod's fierce drive brought Southend's second goal.

reduce the arrears but Zeidler and Piscara missed the best of Union's efforts. Birlem then burst clear for the hosts but just as he was about to shoot at Toone, William Thomson intercepted with a perfect challenge and released 'Dits' Anderson. Anderson stormed upfield and crashed a shot against the Union crossbar. Minutes later King should have completed his hat-trick but blasted over when well placed. Union's best chance of the match came in the eightieth minute when good work by Piscara presented Weisener with an open goal but he contrived to shoot wide of the unguarded Southend net. From the resulting goal kick Southend made it four and King finally completed his hat-trick when, gaining possession from Toone's clearance, he easily beat Union's beleaguered backline and shot past an unprotected Eichelmann.

The whole tour was a resounding success with the Germans being cordial and accommodating hosts. Ironically, six years later, two of Southend's team, Billy Sutherland and Edward 'Dits' Anderson were killed in Belgium defending a trench against the onslaught of the invading German army.

Union Berlin: Eichelmann, Buchmann, Schwarzer, Potsch, Jurga, Steffen, H. Zeidler, Birlem, Weisener, W. Zeidler, Piscara.

Southend United: Percy Toone, Tom Murray, Jerry Thomson, Ernest Emery, Albert Frost, Billy Harrower, Louis Parke, William Sutherland, Alex King, George Harrod, Edward Anderson.

CHELSEA v. SOUTHEND UNITED

11 January 1913   FA Cup First Round

Southend had battled their way through from the preliminary round, overcoming several tough away games, including Cardiff City and Clapton, and facing the notoriously abusive fans at Custom House in London. The reward was a first-round tie against the mighty Chelsea at Stamford Bridge. However, despite a valiant effort, the visitors were condemned to defeat following a poor refereeing performance from Mr Hall of Olton and in particular two highly contentious penalty decisions.

The game was played in horrendous conditions with a continual downpour leaving a disappointing crowd of only 14,000 to witness a tie which was considerably closer than the final scoreline suggested. It was a very dark afternoon and Chelsea decided at the last minute to wear their all-white change strip. Southend's skipper Jerry Thomson won the toss and elected to play up the slight slope but with the wind behind the Shrimpers.

Chelsea's first chance came shortly after kick-off but Harry Ford squandered a good opportunity. Then Chelsea's back Walter Bettridge miscued but his 'keeper spared his blushes as Frost was waiting to pounce. Soon after, Ernie Emery was adjudged to have committed an offence on the edge of his own area but Bob Whittingham's free-kick flashed past Kebbell's post. Southend were then reduced temporarily to ten men when Thomson was off the pitch for some time to receive treatment for a leg injury. Chelsea turned the screw and Billy Kebbell did extremely well to fist a hard drive from Bridgeman over the crossbar. However, the home side took the lead on nineteen minutes when Bridgeman sent a great cross over for Whittingham and his fierce shot saw Kebbell stretching full length to divert the ball onto the post. To his dismay the ball then ricocheted into the side netting on the opposite side of the goal. Kebbell then saved his team with a remarkable stop from England international Vivian Woodward from only three yards out.

Chelsea went two up soon after when Kebbell could only parry Bridgeman's fierce cross and Whittingham was on hand to steer the ball into an unguarded net. Southend players protested that Bridgeman had been offside when he received the ball but the referee turned away their appeals. Chelsea nearly went three up but Billy Brown only found the side netting when well placed. From the goal kick Southend broke forward and Archie Wilson's shot was only half cleared by Brebner's kick. Parke followed up and charged the 'keeper and when both men fell to the ground Albert Frost had the easiest opportunity to reduce the arrears. The half finished with the home side 2-1 up.

The match was decided early in the second half when the referee awarded Chelsea two penalty kicks in quick succession. The first offence was unclear – even the reporters from the London press could not detect an infringement – but following a skirmish in Southend's penalty area the ball was

---

CHELSEA 5
Whittingham (4, 2 pens),
Woodward

SOUTHEND UNITED 2
Frost (2)

Albert Frost
scored both
Southend goals.

cleared, only for the referee to call play back for a spot kick to the home side some moments later. Whittingham duly completed his hat-trick. Moments late Harry Moon was adjudged to have handled another cross from Bridgeman although it was a harsh call as from point-blank range he was unable to move out of the way. Kebbell was beaten again by Whittingham.

Kebbell then held on to a brilliant header from Woodward. It was then Chelsea's turn to suffer from bad luck when Bettridge was forced to retire, leaving them with only ten men. Southend got back in the game when Louis Parke burst clear from Calderhead and attacked the left flank. His cross was flicked on neatly by Bradshaw and then Frost neatly trapped the ball, sidestepped a challenge from Sharp and easily beat Brebner in the home goal.

Southend dominated play and Frost should have completed a hat-trick when Brebner charged out of his goal but missed the ball completely. However the muddy pitch held the ball up and Sharp

The CHELSEA F.C. Chronicle

OFFICIAL PROGRAMME

of

The Chelsea Football & Athletic Company, Limited.

MEMBERS OF

The Football League (Division 1). South Eastern League (Division 1).

(CHAMPIONS, 1909-10. 1911-12.)

Vol. VIII. No. 24.	Saturday, January 11th, 1913.	ONE PENNY. POST FREE 1½d.

A WARNING FROM WALES.

The Cardiff Leek: "Indeed to goodness, don't forget, I've warned you."

(Cardiff City were defeated by Southend, at Cardiff, in the Fifth Qualifying Round.)

was able to get back in time to clear the danger. Southend had a host of chances with the best coming from blistering shots from Emery and Frost. Chelsea, however, put the result beyond all doubt near the end when Woodward ran half the length of the pitch and, evading all challenges, managed to beat Kebbell with a crisp drive. Billy Brown should have scored a sixth in injury time following a bad error from Jack Spencer, but Kebbell again produced a sensational save.

It was a great cup-tie but Southend's luck deserted them and with the foul weather they collected a quarter share, around £240, of a poor gate that was half the seasonal average for the home side.

Chelsea: Ronald Brebner, Walter Bettridge, James Sharp, Fred Taylor, Andrew Ormiston, David Calderhead, Harry Ford, Bob Whittingham, Vivian J. Woodward, William Brown, Billy Bridgeman.

Southend United: Billy Kebbell, Jerry Thomson, Jack Spencer, Ernest Emery, Harry Moon, Charlie Axcell, Fred Scott, Archie Wilson, Albert Frost, Joe Bradshaw, Louis Parke.

Southend United v. Brighton & Hove Albion

Southend had a dream start to life in the new Third Division of the Football League following the election almost en bloc of the entire Southern League First Division.

The Blues' opening fixture in League football saw them with a home tie against old adversaries Brighton & Hove Albion. A glorious sunny day without a cloud in the sky welcomed the club to their new challenge and the board were pleased with the near-10,000 turnout of supporters. The match also saw the opening of a splendid new grandstand at The Kursaal.

Southend opened the encounter at tremendous pace but Brighton's rearguard held firm under a considerable onslaught. It was amusing in the opening exchanges to see the crowd appealing for offside from throw-ins, seemingly unaware of the change of rule which allowed attackers to be 'offside' when receiving a throw-in. New centre forward Albert Fairclough was the outstanding player on the day and he nearly opened the scoring on five minutes when a shot from an excellent cross by Newton went narrowly past the post. Soon after, Nicholls floated in a tempting cross but Fairclough's header was well fielded by Hayes in the Brighton goal.

Southend took the lead after twenty minutes when Wally Little made a bad error and Nicholls' cross was headed firmly into the top right-hand corner by Fairclough for a debut goal. The Shrimpers nearly increased the lead when Fairclough and Myers had chances to score but Hayes' bravery kept his side in the game.

In the fifteen-minute spell up to half-time the visitors had their most productive spell when a well-placed Ted Rodgerson blasted tamely wide and Albion's danger man Jack Doran had a good effort despite clearly handling the ball to bring it under control. In truth though, Tommy Capper's goal was rarely threatened despite conceding four corners, such was the commanding defending of skipper Bob Reid and Jim Henderson.

The second period started in the same vein as the first as Southend laid siege to the visitors' net. Fairclough and Myers squandered several chances to make the game safe. However, the points were secured on sixty-six minutes when Hayes made a save from Fairclough, tipping his shot onto the bar. The ball fell invitingly for Harry Wileman, who controlled the ball and passed sideways to Fairclough who found the roof of the net with some aplomb. Joe Dorsett then had the chance to set up Fairclough for a hat-trick but, instead of passing to his unmarked teammate, Dorsett elected to shoot from an awkward angle and only succeeded in blazing over the bar. Doran then had the ball in the Southend net but the effort was ruled out following a heavy challenge on Tommy Capper.

In the closing moments Southend incredibly hit the bar twice from corner kicks on either side on the pitch by George Nicholls and Joe Dorsett. However, at the close of play, Southend's greater pace and invention meant they were good value for the 2-0 victory.

SOUTHEND UNITED 2   **BRIGHTON & HOVE ALBION 0**
Fairclough (2)

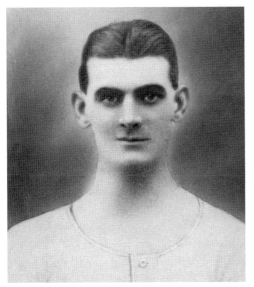 

Above left: Albert Fairclough scored twice on his Blues debut.

Above right: Joe Dorsett could have set up Fairclough for a hat-trick but chose to go it alone.

The record crowd of 9,600 generated receipts of £560. This easily exceeded the previous record by some £170. The watching town mayor added to the club's coffers by contributing £25 to the grandstand fund.

Southend United: Tommy Capper, Bob Reid, Andrew Newton, Harry Wileman, Jim Henderson, Blakey Martin, George Nicholls, Tommy Nuttall, Albert Fairclough, Colin Myers, Joe Dorsett.

Brighton & Hove Albion: Billy Hayes, Jack Woodhouse, Wally Little, Fretwell Hall, Harry Comber, Harry Bentley, Bert Longstaff, George Ritchie, Jack Doran, Ted Rodgerson, Zach March.

Southend United v. Derby County

30 January 1926   FA Cup Fourth Round

With the club less than twenty years old this FA Cup Fourth Round thrashing of unbeaten Second Division leaders Derby County ranked as their finest performance in their fledgling history. Southend had been drawn at home for the fourth straight round having dispatched Dulwich Hamlet (5-1), Gillingham (1-0) and Southport (5-2) in the previous rounds.

The arrival of Derby County, boasting two England internationals in George Thornwell and Harry Storer, caused great excitement in the town and it was no surprise that a new attendance record was set at The Kursaal when 14,225 spectators parted with £1,226, record gate receipts, to watch the spectacle. In truth, even the most ardent of Southend supporters were predicting a troubled afternoon for the Shrimpers, with the exception of Herbert Upton of Westcliff, who claimed to have 'at least fifty Westcliff residents' who would attest to his correct forecasting of the final result. The omens, however, were not good for the home side as regular inside right Jim Bissett pulled out at the last minute due the sudden death of his brother. Fred Graver was drafted in as a late replacement and put in a Man-of-the-Match performance as Derby were swept away down by the seafront.

The match kicked off with tremendous noise from the Kursaal crowd, so noisy in fact that residents of Hadleigh some five miles away could hear the cheering! The opening period was even but Southend took a shock lead after seventeen minutes when Jack Andrews scored from outside the penalty area. More chances came Southend's way, with Billy Hick squandering opportunities to increase the home side's advantage. However, the Blues went two up in the thirty-fifth minute when Graver punished indecision in the Derby rearguard to shoot home with aplomb. The dominating Southend performance was greeting with a standing ovation at half-time when the Shrimpers reached the break two goals to the good.

Remarkably, Southend went 3-0 up after sixty-five minutes when Billy Hick, the lone striker in a 4-5-1 formation, skilfully dribbled past Harry Wightman before having the tenacity to round Derby's goalkeeper Ben Olney and slip the ball into an unguarded net. With seventy-one minutes on the clock Southend went further ahead when Billy Hick, looking suspiciously offside, took advantage of Derby's hesitancy to race clear and beat Olney for a second time in six minutes. Six minutes later Derby scored a consolation goal when Lionel Murphy's speculative cross seemed to get caught in the wind and drifted over Billy Moore's head into the Southend net.

The incredible victory made national headlines but it was the visitors' hometown press that was most scathing of County's inept performance. The *Derby Daily Express* described it as 'the last word in shocks' and the *Derby Telegraph* stated that 'Southend were supremely indifferent to the greatness of the opposition and fought with tremendous enthusiasm'.

SOUTHEND UNITED 4   **DERBY COUNTY 1**
  Hick (2), Andrews,   Murphy
  Graver

SOUTHEND UNITED *v.* DERBY COUNTY

Fred Graver (*above right*) was a late call-up to the team but turned in a Man-of-the-Match performance.

Southend went out in the fifth round to Nottingham Forest by a slim 1-0 defeat in front of another record gate of 18,153 at The Kursaal. Ernest Mongford, a wealthy supporter and local businessman, rewarded Ted Birnie and his squad of players with an all-expenses-paid evening of food and dancing at the National Supporters Club to thank the team on behalf of the town for some tremendous entertainment.

Southend United: Billy Moore, Jack French, Tommy Sayles, Fred Jewhurst, Frank O'Rawe, Jack Andrews, Hughie Morris, Fred Graver, Billy Hick, Bill Shaw, Steve Smith.
Derby County: Ben Olney, Harry Wightman, Archie Ritchie, John McIntyre, Harry Thoms, Syd Plackett, George Thornwell, Frank Keetley, Harry Bedford, Harry Storer, Lionel Murphy.

Clapton Orient v. Southend United

6 December 1930   Football League Third Division (South)

Southend United's only ever visit to the famous twin towers of Wembley Stadium came in the most unusual of circumstances.

Their away fixture at Clapton Orient's Lea Bridge Road stadium was moved to Wembley as Orient's ground had been closed following a bad injury to a Torquay United player resulting from the close proximity of the pitch barrier to the playing surface. While remedial work was carried out the East Londoners were forced to hire the national stadium in order to stage two home games. The first resulted in an easy 3-0 win over Brentford in front of a healthy 8,000-plus crowd. However, the visit of Southend United attracted a crowd of only 1,916, which must have looked very odd in the vast stadium with a then capacity of 100,000.

However, the Southend side turned in a distinctly unmemorable performance at the famous stadium. It should be said that Ted Birnie's team selection was something of an experiment following the FA Cup exit at the hands of Torquay the previous weekend. He dramatically dropped skipper Tommy Dixon and brought in young Bob Ward. Furthermore, Donoven moved to inside left and Johnson took over at left half. Arthur Crompton, despite being right footed, was seconded to the outside left berth.

Southend had a good first half, however, and had plenty of chances before scoring in the twenty-fifth minute. Southend gained a corner and Fred Barnett launched a deep kick into the O's penalty area. Jimmy Shankly's deft header back allowed Mickey Jones the easiest of chances to nod the ball over the line from close range with Orient 'keeper Harry Blackwell unsighted among a ruck of players. In the next period of play Shankly skimmed the crossbar twice and Barnett had a powerful shot cannon back off the upright.

This was an equaliser following Clapton's early breakthrough when a rare fumble by Billy Moore in the Southend goal allowed Jack Fowler to open the scoring into a virtually unguarded goal. The veteran forward was a constant thorn in the visitors' side with his drive and clever play, and a vital factor was Bob Ward's nervousness in tackling the powerful Orient forward.

Into the second half and the Blues nearly took the lead through Dickie Donoven. His first effort was a speculative long-range effort which caught Blackwell off guard in the Orient net. He was mightily relieved to see the ball just clear his crossbar. Then a Donoven corner slipped out of Blackwell's hands and was just about to cross the line when Ernie Morley managed to hook the ball to safety. However, Southend's downfall came when Crompton, their best player in the opening period, was strangely neglected in the second half. This meant the side lost its shape and creativity and the home side took control of the encounter.

The O's took the lead on sixty-seven minutes. Johnson misjudged a challenge and Reg Tricker easily converted a one-on-one opportunity against Moore. The clinching goal came on seventy-three

---

CLAPTON ORIENT 3   **SOUTHEND UNITED 1**

Fowler (2), Tricker   Jones

Above left: Wembley scorer Emlyn 'Mickey' Jones.

minutes and was shrouded in controversy. Tricker played a through ball for Fowler who was clearly offside but both the referee and the linesman failed to award the decision and, while the Southend rearguard appealed and waited for a whistle, Fowler all but walked the ball into an empty net. Shankly had a late chance to reduce the arrears but the side had already suffered a fatal body blow. The dubious offside call ensured that the club's only visit to Wembley would be marked with a defeat.

Clapton Orient: Harry Blackwell, Ernie Morley, Billy Broadbent, Eddie Lawrence, Jack Galbraith, Jim Bolton, Rollo Jack, Arthur Cropper, Reg Tricker, Jack Fowler, Jack Fletcher.
Southend United: Billy Moore, Jack French, Dave Robinson, Bob Ward, Joe Wilson, Joe Johnson, Fred Barnett, Mickey Jones, Jimmy Shankly, Dickie Donoven, Arthur Crompton.

Southend United v. Golders Green

24 November 1934   FA Cup First Round

Southend hit double figures for the first time since their early years and some breathtaking footwork put the amateurs from North London to the sword. A healthy crowd of 8,500 paid receipts of £531 and included a sizeable contingent of visiting supporters, who arrived on specially chartered trains from Cricklewood and Hampstead Heath.

Southend attacked from the kick-off and within the first minute secured a penalty kick when referee Mr Brown had no option but to penalise Bucci for handling Bert Oswald's cross. However, Harry Lane's weak kick was cleared by the outstretched right foot of the Golders Green 'keeper Gooding. The visitors rallied and attacked with some vigour but Billy Moore kept the Southend net intact with a string of good saves. However, despite the even nature of the opening exchanges the floodgates opened in the twenty-fourth minute when Billy Carr's neat pass found Fred Cheesmur with his back to goal. His flick split the defence and Harry Johnson found the net with ease. A similar move two minutes later saw Jimmy Deacon release Cheesmur and his excellent touch gave himself the simplest of chances to increase the Shrimpers' advantage. In the final moments of the opening half Southend made it 3-0 when Jimmy Deacon's header beat Gooding following an accurate centre from Harry Lane.

Although Southend had taken their chances well the half-time score was a little flattering as Golders Green's wide men Drinkwater and Breagan had given Morfitt and Kelly a torrid time and the visitors' amateur international Freddy Evans had tested Billy Moore on several occasions but was generally well marshalled by Joe Wilson. Golders Green half-back Richardson was injured early on in a collision with Deacon but after treatment for a bad cut over his right eye he resumed his place in defence. However, the odd gap in the visiting rearguard became gaping holes in the second half as Southend's forwards ran riot. Minutes into the restart Richardson upended Johnson and a second penalty was awarded. Following Lane's earlier miss, Billy Carr was handed the spot kick and despite another poor kick, Gooding's touch could not keep the ball out of the net.

The fifth goal came courtesy of Harry Lane although it was something of a fluke. Oswald's corner was weakly fisted away by Gooding, and the ball literally rolled down Lane's leg, hit his foot and crossed the line. Number six came when Gooding made his first real clanger when he dropped a simple catch into the path of Johnson who again scored with ease. The outstanding Cheesmur displayed outrageous skill in creating the seventh when he trapped the ball with his foot, flicked it up onto his chest and then headed over his marker into the path of the grateful Johnson. Having scored a hat-trick himself Johnson then turned provider, slipping the ball through for Cheesmur to net number eight. However, with the goals raining in, all the Southend players pushed up in search of more but the visitors' best player, Drinkwater, took advantage of poor marking to register a consolation strike.

SOUTHEND UNITED 10	GOLDERS GREEN 1
Johnson (5), Cheesmur (2), Deacon, Carr (pen), Lane	Drinkwater

SOUTHEND UNITED v. GOLDERS GREEN

Above left: Harry Lane missed a first-minute penalty but contributed to the fifth Southend goal in this double-figure rout.

Above right: Southend United team group for the 1934/35 season.

The ninth and tenth were scored by Harry Johnson. The ninth was a result of an under-weighted back pass, which Johnson easily collected and rounded the 'keeper to shoot into an unguarded net. The tenth came late on when Oswald centred, Cheesmur dummied Broadis, and Johnson swept the ball home.

So the club achieved its record competitive victory as a Football League club, which has subsequently been equalled twice but never beaten. As for the routed visitors, they later changed their name to Hendon.

Southend United: Billy Moore, Jack Morfitt, Lawrie Kelly, Norman Mackay, Joe Wilson, Billy Carr, Harry Lane, Harry Johnson, Fred Cheesmur, Jimmy Deacon, Bert Oswald.

Golders Green: Gooding, Boston, Richardson, White, Broadis, Bucci, Breagan, Edwards, F. Evans, T. Evans, Drinkwater.

TOTTENHAM HOTSPUR v. SOUTHEND UNITED

11 January 1936   FA Cup Third Round

The Shrimpers had already dispatched Newport County and Burton Albion, the latter with an impressive 5-0 beating at the Southend Stadium, when they were handed a tough third-round tie away to then-Second Division Tottenham Hotspur.

Spurs were managed by Jack Tresadern, a former England international and a veteran of the first Wembley FA Cup final when he played for West Ham against Bolton Wanderers. The London outfit also boasted England player Arthur Rowe and such well-known names as Vic Buckingham and Les Howe, who between them would clock up 600 appearances for Tottenham. Also in their line-up was inside right Sam Bell, who would later play 70-odd games for Southend before his career was interrupted by the Second World War.

Southend entered the game as rank underdogs but took a shock lead just four minutes in when Spurs' rearguard failed to deal with a deft through ball from Leo Stevens and Channell only succeeded in deflecting the ball into the path of Len Bolan, who neatly dispatched his shot past an onrushing Percy Hooper. Ten minutes later Spurs had a golden opportunity to repair the damage when Bell was felled in the penalty area by a clumsy challenge from Dave Robinson. However, Southend's Irish international custodian, George Mackenzie, pulled off a smart save diving full length to his right. However, on seventeen minutes the scores were level when some scrappy Blues defending gave Johnny Morrison the chance to prod the ball into the Southend net. Minutes later the Shrimpers were behind when veteran full-back Robinson made a complete hash of a clearance and Fred Sargent had the simple task of beating Mackenzie from close range. The half continued with the Blues pushing for an equaliser and just before half-time a great run by Bert Oswald resulted in a deep cross into the danger area which allowed Len Bolan to head home a well-deserved leveller.

The second half started with the Shrimpers laying siege to the Paxton Road End and after fifty minutes Southend went 3-2 up when Oswald produced another devastating cross, which was badly fumbled by Hooper in the Spurs goal. His spill gave the easiest of chances to Bolan to complete a memorable hat-trick by prodding the ball into an unguarded net. Southend then sat back on their lead and tried to absorb some tremendous pressure from the Londoners. However, on sixty-four minutes Spurs levelled again when Sargent scored with an unstoppable drive from outside the penalty area. Les Howe had the chance to put Spurs ahead but his blistering shot was superbly parried by Mackenzie. Unfortunately the ball came back into play off the post and fell straight into the path of Morrison who slotted home to make the score 4-3 to Tottenham.

With time running out Southend committed more players forward in search of an equaliser. Leo Stevens barged his way into the penalty area and with the Spurs backline in total confusion Harry

---

TOTTENHAM HOTSPUR 4   **SOUTHEND UNITED 4**

Sargent (2), Morrison (2)   Bolan (3), Lane

Above: Len Bolan scored a hat-trick against mighty Spurs.

Lane scored to give the Blues a money-spinning replay at the Southend Stadium. A large crowd of 48,839 watched the 4-4 thriller at White Hart Lane.

The replay took place on the following Wednesday afternoon, when a frosty pitch made playing conditions tricky and Spurs overcame Southend by a narrow 2-1 margin, Bolan again scoring for Southend with Sargeant and Willie Evans netting for Tottenham. The clash was watched by a record gate at the Southend Stadium of 22,862, which generated record receipts of £1,971. Spurs enjoyed a good FA Cup run but eventually went out to Sheffield United in a sixth-round tie at Bramall Lane.

Tottenham Hotspur: Percy Hooper, Fred Channell, Vic Buckingham, Les Howe, Arthur Rowe, Ernie Phypers, Fred Sargent, Andy Duncan, Johnny Morrison, Sam Bell, Willie Evans.

Southend United: George Mackenzie, Jimmy Nelson, Dave Robinson, Jimmy Deacon, Charlie Turner, Billy Carr, Len Bolan, Fred Cheesmur, Leo Stevens, Harry Lane, Bert Oswald.

Ipswich Town v. Southend United

27 August 1938   Football League Third Division (South)

Ipswich Town had won election to the Football League as champions of the Southern League and after a substantial spending spree in the close season, which dwarfed the budget of their new counterparts, looked to take the Third Division (South) by storm.

Their opening match was a home game against the Shrimpers and the visitors took the opportunity of fine weather to arrive at the Suffolk town by boat chartered from the end of the pier. However, the players must have lost their sea legs en route as they turned in a very poor first-half performance and gifted the newcomers a goal after only three minutes. Southend, playing in unfamiliar red shirts, were pegged back from the start but a quick break saw Tudor Martin hit the bar with a fierce drive. From the clearance by Billy Dale, Fred Jones and Jack Trainer jockeyed for control. Trainer had the chance to head the ball back to his 'keeper but failed to do so. Mackenzie, an Irish international, was left in no man's land and tried in vain to catch the bouncing ball. His miss allowed Jones the easiest of tap-ins into an unguarded net.

Ipswich dominated play but only added to their lead a minute before half-time when Jones found Gilbert Alsop in an unmarked position and his well-timed shot beat Mackenzie with ease. Earlier the majority of the 20,700 crowd had bayed for a penalty kick when a cross from Williams was headed goalwards by Bryn Davies and hit Trainer. However the referee, Mr Stevens, adjudged the ball to have struck Trainer's chest rather than his arm.

The outcome was put beyond reasonable doubt forty seconds after the restart when a bad error from Billy Carr under pressure from Davies and Jones allowed the latter to secure his second goal of the game. However, rather than collapse completely after this setback, the visitors rallied with tremendous spirit and Town had their 'keeper, Mick Burns, to thank for a string of fine saves.

Billy Carr nearly atoned for his earlier mistake when his header from a Bert Oswald corner was tipped around the post. Sid Bell then hit a powerful rising shot which was touched over the bar by Burns. However, Southend reduced the arrears in the fifty-seventh minute when Billy Bushby scored an exceptional goal. He picked up the ball well outside the penalty area and deftly went past McLuckie before unleashing a powerful shot that Burns could get a hand to but was unable to prevent from finding the back of the net. However, the three-goal cushion was restored just three minutes later when some poor Southend marking allowed Jones to drift into the danger area, draw Mackenzie out of position before finding Bryn Davies unmarked to tap in number four.

To the credit of the visitors they rallied again and from the kick-off gained a corner kick. Oswald floated in a beautiful ball that allowed Bushby to head home for a second goal. The Southend forwards poured forward in search of more goals and Ipswich were forced to defend stoutly. Bolan clashed heads with McLuckie in one skirmish, with the latter needing attention to patch up a deep

---

IPSWICH TOWN 4   **SOUTHEND UNITED 2**

Jones (2), Alsop, Davies   Bushby (2)

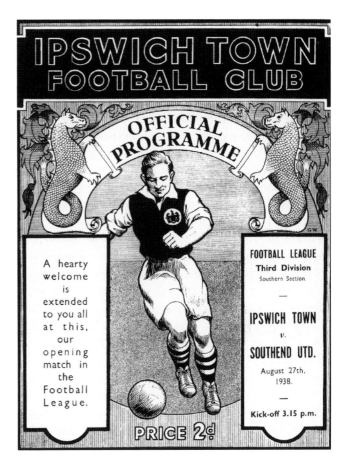

Above: Billy Bushby scored twice for the Shrimpers.

gash on his balding pate. However, the Shrimpers' hopes of a dramatic finish were scuppered when their most dangerous forward, Bushby, was reduced to the role of limping passenger on the wing following an unnecessarily heavy challenge by Tom Fillingham.

The Luton-based referee was praised for his handling of a bruising but entertaining game. The town centre shops were festooned in Ipswich colours and even the ball boys were dressed in blue and white hats. It all made for a memorable encounter and Southend had taken 2,000 supporters to Portman Road with eight charabancs coming from Essex as well as hundreds of cars. Many supporters had followed the lead of the team and arrived by sea.

Ipswich Town: Mick Burns, Billy Dale, Ossie Parry, George Perrett, Tom Fillingham, Jimmy McLuckie, Jackie Williams, Bryn Davies, Fred Jones, Gilbert Alsop, Jackie Little.

Southend United: George Mackenzie, Johnny Milne, Billy Forster, Billy Leighton, Jack Trainer, Billy Carr, Len Bolan, Billy Bushby, Tudor Martin, Sid Bell, Bert Oswald.

SOUTHEND UNITED v. CHESTERFIELD

This dramatic match was the culmination of an epic three-game FA Cup third-round tie. Southend had progressed to that stage with a 3-0 victory over the famous amateur side Corinthians, with Alf Smirk netting a hat-trick. This was followed by a tight 1-0 victory at Port Vale in the second round. Blues' reward was a fairly mundane-looking tie away to Second Division Chesterfield.

The first game was staged on 7 January when Britain was in the grip of a very harsh winter. Chesterfield's Saltergate ground was snowbound and in an attempt to get the game played the Spireites' board hired local unemployed labourers to clear snow from the pitch and terraces. Numerous coke braziers were rented to try and thaw the frozen pitch out. However, an upsurge in temperature overnight saw the pitch reduced to a boggy swamp. Now left with the task of trying to dry the pitch out, the club dumped tonnes of building sand onto the worst-affected areas in a last-ditch attempt to get the game played.

The referee, Regimental Sergeant-Major Green, arrived at the ground at around one o'clock and declared the pitch playable. However, in the run up to kick-off Saltergate was enveloped in a dense fog. The match was tied at 1-1 with goals from James Spedding for the home side and a spectacular sixty-first-minute equaliser from Keith Hague, when after seventy-three minutes the match was abandoned due to the ever-thickening fog.

The game was restaged the following Wednesday afternoon when a fresh covering of snow over the mud and sand had left the pitch with a three-inch layer of slush. Again the same referee declared the pitch fit, and a hard-fought match ended all square at 1-1. Tom Lyon had given the Spireites the lead just eight minutes from full time but Billy Bushby levelled only two minutes later to send the tie back to the Southend Stadium for a replay.

The replay was staged on the following Tuesday afternoon when a crowd of 11,393 assembled to witness an incredible match. The Shrimpers tore into Chesterfield from the kick-off and were two goals to the good inside twelve minutes. A slick move of crisp passing allowed Billy Bushby to open the scoring and shortly after Len Bolan slotted home from a centre from Alf Smirk. However, the visitors rallied in the second half and Tom Lyon reduced the arrears with a powerful shot. Nine minutes later Chesterfield were level when Jack Hughes found the net after Mackenzie had parried superbly from Milligan.

With no addition to the score in the normal ninety minutes the match went into extra time. In the first fifteen-minute period former Spurs inside forward Sam 'Sid' Bell scored twice for the Shrimpers. His first was a powerful shot that cannoned off Chesterfield's half-back William Kidd and left their goalkeeper Ray Middleton wrong footed. The second was a neat finish from a flick-on by Bushby.

SOUTHEND UNITED 4   **CHESTERFIELD 3**
  Bell (2), Bushby, Bolan   Lyon, Hughes, Milburn (pen)

SOUTHEND UNITED v. CHESTERFIELD

Right: Sid Bell scored twice against the Spireites.

Far right: Programme from the abandoned first match.

In the 112th minute, with Southend having a seemingly unassailable 4-2 lead, RSM Green awarded Chesterfield a vehemently disputed penalty when Ernie Stokes was adjudged to have handled the ball. George Milburn easily beat Mackenzie from the spot kick. The decision incensed the home crowd but worse was to come when in stoppage time Kidd charged the Southend 'keeper to the ground. Mackenzie jumped up and jostled the Chesterfield player and incredibly the referee awarded a second penalty to the visitors. The Southend players and crowd erupted in fury and the game was held up for some time due to the protestations. Len Bolan was dismissed for swearing at the linesman and Sid Bell and Alf Smirk were cautioned for dissent and ungentlemanly conduct, the latter for throwing mud at Milburn as he tried to take the spot kick! With order restored Milburn, evidently put off by the delay, shot weakly and Mackenzie saved low down to his right.

The crowd invaded the pitch at the final whistle and a hefty police escort ensured the referee came to no harm from a furious crowd although on police advice he was confined to his dressing room while the mob dispersed.

The referee's report ensured three Southend players, Bolan, Smirk and Bell, were summoned to Lancaster Gate on 6 February to explain their actions. All three pleaded guilty to misconduct and were each fined £3, with Bolan also being banned for seven days.

Southend United: George Mackenzie, Johnny Milne, Ernie Stokes, Arthur Harris, Keith Hague, Bob Jackson, Alf Smirk, Len Bolan, Billy Bushby, Sid Bell, Tudor Martin.

Chesterfield: Ray Middleton, George Milburn, William Kidd, Walter McMillen, Jack Seagrave, Eric Weightman, Jack Hughes, Tom Lyon, Dudley Milligan, James Spedding, Les Sullivan.

Bristol Rovers v. Southend United

5 October 1946   Football League Third Division (South)

A routine-looking visit to Eastville provided one of the most bizarre matches and incredible victories in the long history of Southend United. An amazing bout of ill fortune left Harry Warren's match plans in tatters and the United dressing room resembling a hospital ward.

The travelling party left the town at 8 a.m. to assure themselves an early arrival at Paddington to catch the 11.15 a.m. train to Bristol. The club had reserved a carriage and ordered lunch but just before departure an apologetic guard told Warren that the train had no restaurant car and food would not be available. A mad scrabble ensured some sandwiches were obtained but the team would have to face their opponents on virtually empty stomachs.

After the train had just passed through Reading a game of whist was disturbed by the sound of shattering glass. Southend's goalkeeper, Ted 'Gunner' Hankey had attempted to shut a window that would not budge and when more force was applied the pane shattered and quarter-inch-thick glass lacerated Hankey arms and hands with one hand deeply cut. With Hankey on the verge of collapsing, Warren and trainer Wilf Copping managed to stem the bleeding and Hankey bravely said he would still be able to play although the task looked impossible.

On arrival at Bristol station Hankey was escorted to a nearby hospital and his injuries attended to and his hand sewn up. The team had decided en route to keep the disaster to themselves. On arrival at the stadium it was then tradition for the home officials to ask for team changes to the one previously notified for the programme. Remarkably no one asked and the tannoy announcer read out an unchanged line-up with Hankey in goal. Southend did not feel any obligation to say otherwise and hand a considerable advantage to their opponents.

It had been decided that Bob Jackson, a full-back, would play in goal and his place in defence would be taken by Stan Montgomery, who insisted on playing against doctors orders.

In the opening exchanges a catalogue of injuries occurred to the makeshift side. Sheard was limping and was forced to play on the wing, Harris pulled a leg muscle, Smirk sustained a cut to the eye which needed three stitches and Thompson was badly shaken following a hefty challenge. However, Jackson was brilliant in goal and, wearing Hankey's trademark cap, fooled everyone into thinking he was the regular custodian. Rovers opened the scoring on twenty-one minutes when a vicious swerving shot from left-winger Idris Lewis exposed Jackson's lack of height and found the top corner of the net.

The vistors showed tremendous spirit and rallied to take the lead within five minutes of the setback. Firstly Joe Sibley burst through the home defence before squaring to Smirk, who levelled the scores. Moments later Sheard launched a counterattack with a clearing header that found Frank Dudley. His sublime through ball found Cyril Thompson who outpaced the defenders around him

---

BRISTOL ROVERS 1   **SOUTHEND UNITED 3**

Lewis   Smirk, Thompson (2)

Bristol Rovers v. Southend United

Bob Jackson's remarkable performance as emergency goalkeeper fooled the opposition and the press reporters.

SOUTHEND UNITED. — Hankey; Jackson, Linton; Harris, Sheard, Montgomery; Sibley, Smirke, Dudley, Thompson, Lane.

Referee: W. E. Ross-Gower (London).

The Rovers, playing in red and white jerseys, soon forced their opponents on the defensive by enterprising play. Pitt sent in a nice shot, but Hankey caught and cleared.

He accepted a pass from Carr, cut in, and drove in a hard ground shot, but Hankey did well in goal.

The first time that Southend got away Sibley, a forceful winger, worried Weare, who held on to the ball and cleared.

He once cleverly beat two opponents, but instead of passing he drove in a hard shot from a difficult angle. Hankey again came to the rescue of the visitors.

From one, Lambden sent in a header, but Hankey slipped the ball over the bar.

The Southend defenders had far more work to do than had the Rovers' defence but Hankey was never worried, though Lambden was always in attendance.

and shot home. Incredibly Southend scored a third after thirty-two minutes when clever play by Smirk released Thompson again and his thunderous shot went over the head of Rovers' 'keeper Jack Weare and dipped in just below the crossbar.

The second half saw Rovers encamped in the visitors' half of the field, and with a crocked team Southend rarely got out of their own half. However, despite wave after wave of attacks and shots raining in on his goal Jackson stood firm and denied at least six clear-cut goalscoring opportunities with amazing bravery.

The majority of the 9,000 crowd, unaware of the real story, loudly applauded the Shrimpers off the field at the end of the game. Ted Hankey could not contain himself and went bounding onto the pitch at the end, hands heavily bandaged, to congratulate Jackson on his heroics.

Rovers' manager Brough Fletcher was so respectful of his opponents' performance, and particularly that of 'Hankey' in goal, that he took a gift of a large box of cigarettes to the visitors dressing room only to 'nearly collapse' when Harry Warren revealed the true extent of the adversity his side had overcome.

Bristol Rovers: Jack Weare, George Peacock, Barry Watkins, Harry Bamford, Ray Warren, Wilf Whitfield, George Petherbridge, Jack Pitt, Vic Lambden, Lance Carr, Idris Lewis.

Southend United: Bob Jackson, Stan Montgomery, Tommy Linton, Arthur Harris, Frank Sheard, Frank Walton, Joe Sibley, Alf Smirk, Frank Dudley, Cyril Thompson, Harry Lane.

BARNET v. SOUTHEND UNITED

Southend destroyed the non-leaguers in this FA Cup second-round tie and with it chalked up the club's record away win. Despite scoring nine goals, incredibly Southend's rampant forwards struck the Barnet woodwork on six occasions and the final score should have been well into double figures.

The game was played in bad conditions, thick fog descending before the game and Barnet's sloping pitch, known locally as the mud-heap, lived up to its reputation. The *Standard* reporter 'The Onlooker' commented that it would have been better to play the match on Southend's foreshore, such was the state of the Underhill pitch.

The crowd was just short of a new ground record at 8,065 but nearly half came from Southend and one enterprising individual took a brisk trade outside the ground with his stall of blue and white Southend 'favours'.

Southend kicked off with great fervour and gained three corners in the opening two minutes. Barnet successfully repelled the attacks but could do little to prevent the opening goal on seven minutes. It was scored by Harry Lane, whose initial shot struck the bar and bounced down to Alf Smirk who returned the ball to Lane. He made no mistake this time, burying the shot in the corner of Powell's net. A minute later it was 2-0 when Cyril Thompson powered home Smirk's accurate cross. A whitewash looked on the cards but the home side rallied and took control for a short spell and reduced the arrears when some clever play by Kelleher drew Sheard out of position and allowed Phipps to drive the ball past Hankey. However, Southend reasserted themselves and went 3-1 up in the twenty-ninth minute when Lane converted a neat cross from Smirk. Six minutes later Lane completed his hat-trick following some clever play by Joe Sibley. Roles were reversed for goal number five just before half-time, when Sibley headed home Lane's corner kick.

The vistors went 6-1 up just two minutes after the restart when Ken Bennett was in place to react quickest to a Thompson shot that cannoned back off the crossbar. Then from the kick-off Smirk robbed Kelleher of the ball and sent in one of his trademark swerving crosses, which Barnet's half-back Bunker could only slice into his own net.

The eighth goal came in the fifty-seventh minute when some dazzling wing play from Harry Lane released Cyril Thompson for an easy score. Shortly after, Barnet were reduced to ten men when Reilly and Linton tussled for a loose ball. Reilly badly jarred his leg and was unable to continue.

Despite their numerical disadvantage Barnet then scored again when some shoddy marking allowed Phipps to score his second when faced with a virtually open goal. Southend's ninth came seven minutes from the end when Bennett completed the rout. However, despite the scoreline it was reported that Barnet's clever forwards gave the Shrimpers rearguard a hard time and Hankey and his backs Walton and Linton had more work to do than the scoreline would suggest.

BARNET 2

Phipps (2)

SOUTHEND UNITED 9

Lane (3), Thompson, Sibley (2),
Bennett (2), Bunker (o.g.)

Above: Joe Sibley scored two of Southend's nine goals against Barnet.

The match was played with great sportsmanship, with the trainers only coming onto the pitch as a result of the accidental collision that led to Reilly's early departure. Barnet, holders of the FA Amateur Cup, were the last amateur team left in the competition and took their beating well and sportingly wished Southend good luck for the rest of the season.

Despite the atrocious conditions, the mist not clearing until the closing moments, Southend made light of the muddy pitch and played some brilliant football that was described in some reports as 'dazzling'.

Barnet: Powell, Bunker, Hawkins, Gerrans, Leek, Pymm, Finch, Kelleher, Phipps, Hawkes, Reilly.
Southend United: Ted Hankey, Tommy Linton, Frank Walton, Arthur Harris, Frank Sheard, Stan Montgomery, Joe Sibley, Alf Smirk, Cyril Thompson, Ken Bennett, Harry Lane.

SOUTHEND UNITED v. SWINDON TOWN

24 February 1951   Football League Third Division (South)

The Southend players were still smarting from a 3-0 exit from the FA Cup at the hands of the Robins in November when the sides faced each other at Roots Hall for this Third Division (South) encounter. A crowd of over 10,000 came to watch the game but the majority were shocked to see the home side two down inside the first fourteen minutes.

The visitors started strongly and took the lead just six minutes in when Roy Onslow scored with a fierce thirty-yard shot that gave Tommy Scannell no chance in the Southend goal. Billy Millar nearly doubled their advantage a minute later but Scannell pulled off a spectacular save. Southend broke downfield and won a free-kick close to the penalty area. Sandy Anderson's effort nearly went in but 'keeper Norman Uprichard, who would later join the Blues, just got the ball to safety.

Swindon's second goal came in the fourteenth minute when an inch-perfect cross from Harry Lunn was met by Maurice Owen, who scored with ease. Four minutes later Tommy Tippett reduced the arrears and he scored the goals that would turn the game on its head. Gifted skipper Jimmy McAlinden gathered the ball in midfield and, after beating two players, found Joe Sibley in space. Sibley's accurate centre found Tippett in an ideal place to score from close range.

Twenty minutes gone and Southend were back on level terms when a short back pass was intercepted by Reg Davies and, despite a brave effort from Uprichard, he slotted the ball into an unguarded net. The third Southend goal came in the twenty-third minute when another scintillating move between McAlinden and Sibley resulted in another great cross that Cyril Grant headed into the net.

Jimmy Lawler registered Southend's next goal after thirty-two minutes when Swindon managed to clear a corner kick. Lawler met the ball sweetly and the shot deflected in off full-back Billy Lloyd. Southend were now in total domination of proceedings and a fifth goal came before half-time when another centre from Sibley found Davies in space and his accurate centre was rifled home by Grant.

Two minutes after the restart and it was 6-2 when Jimmy McAlinden, an irresistible force, stormed forward and lofted the ball into the area and Reg Davies applied the finishing touch with a smart header.

Tommy Tippett scored his second and Southend's seventh after sixty-one minutes when Sibley found McAlinden on the edge of the penalty area and his drive rebounded to Tippett, who scored with ease. Tippett's hat-trick came three minutes later when he drilled in yet another accurate centre from the electric Joe Sibley.

SOUTHEND UNITED 8   **SWINDON TOWN 2**

Tippett (3), Davies (2),   Onslow, Owen
Grant (2), Lawler

SOUTHEND UNITED V. SWINDON TOWN

Above: Tommy Tippett bagged a hat-trick in this amazing match.

It was strange that after such a prolific bout of scoring the final twenty-five minutes were goalless. The Shrimpers were certain Tippett's shot crossed the line in the last minute but the referee waved play on.

This was a truly breathtaking performance from a Southend team that seemed to be able to score goals whenever they wanted to.

Southend United: Tommy Scannell, Joe Loughran, Sandy Anderson, Jackie French, Jim Stirling, Jimmy Lawler, Joe Sibley, Jimmy McAlinden, Cyril Grant, Reg Davies, Tommy Tippett.
Swindon Town: Norman Uprichard, Billy Lloyd, Harry May, Harry Kaye, Garth Hudson, Eddie Batchelor, Harry Lunn, Roy Onslow, Maurice Owen, Billy Millar, Jimmy Bain.

EVERTON v. SOUTHEND UNITED

8 January 1955   FA Cup Third Round

This match was watched by a crowd of 53,043, which remains the largest gate ever to watch a Southend United game, and the Shrimpers' share of the gate was a healthy £1,400. It was a remarkable encounter in many ways and Southend perhaps deserved a replay, as it was generally accepted that the home side were not two goals better than their less illustrious visitors. Southend were forced to play the last twelve minutes with ten men when Ken Bainbridge limped off despite having a painkilling injection at half-time.

Southend were skippered by Kevin Baron, who received a warm welcome from the home supporters who remembered his times with Liverpool. However, they were not so happy after three minutes when Baron gave the visitors a shock lead. Southend won a corner when Baron dispossessed Cyril Lello and found Hollis in space but a brilliant tackle from Tommy Jones forced a corner kick. Bainbridge swung the ball into the area and Jimmy O'Neill jumped to pluck the ball out of the air but Baron beat him to it and headed into the net.

The Toffees should have equalised three minutes later when Harry Threadgold could only push out a centre from Wally Fielding. The loose ball fell invitingly for Irish international Tommy Eglington but he shot hopelessly wide with the goal gaping. Minutes later Ken Bainbridge picked up the injury that would consign him to a passenger role for the rest of the game. He strained his back and badly pulled a thigh muscle in a challenge with Wainwright and he bravely hobbled on after lengthy treatment from trainer Dave Robinson.

Bainbridge would have certainly scored in the tenth minute but for his injury, when Sibley's cross was fumbled by O'Neill and fell into the path of Bainbridge. However, he could not reach the ball in time and the chance was gone. O'Neill's shaky start continued when he made a mess of a Roy Hollis shot but was grateful for the heavy mud that held the ball up sufficiently for him to recover and dive on the ball right on the goal line.

The Southend rearguard was generally coping well although Bill Pavitt was being given a hard time by the pacy Eglington. Everton equalised on twenty-two minutes when Wainwright's cross was headed into the danger area by Eglington. Threadgold and Harry Potts went up for the ball and Potts managed to nod the ball over the 'keeper's head.

The thrilling football continued and the home side took the lead through fortunate circumstances a minute before half-time. Wally Fielding showed some dazzling footwork and sent in a powerful shot from thirty yards. Threadgold looked to have the shot covered but the ball took a wicked deflection off Sandy Anderson and rocketed into the net.

After the restart the visitors shook the home crowd again when after some brilliant work from Baron, Sibley looked certain to score. His well-struck drive, however, went just past the post. Soon

EVERTON 3	SOUTHEND UNITED 1
Potts, Fielding, Hickson	Baron

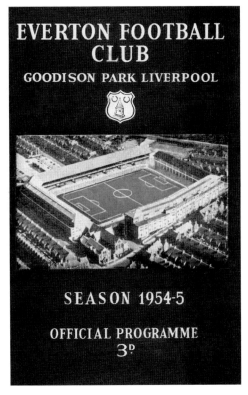

EVERTON FOOTBALL CLUB

GOODISON PARK LIVERPOOL

SEASON 1954-5

OFFICIAL PROGRAMME 3ᴰ

Above left: Liverpudlian Kevin Baron gave Southend a shock lead at Goodison Park.

after, Goodison Park was engulfed in a thick fog, which made conditions difficult although Southend continued to attack, Bill Pavitt whistling a shot just over the crossbar from long range. Everton's third goal came on sixty-eight minutes when a breathtaking move between Lello, Eglington and Potts found burly striker Dave Hickson well placed to drive the ball into the net. Southend tried valiantly to get back into the game but Everton's rearguard slammed the door shut.

The visitors were awarded a generous ovation from the home crowd who were more than relieved to hear the final whistle after a titanic battle.

Everton: Jimmy O'Neill, Eric Moore, Peter Farrell, Cyril Lello, Eddie Wainwright, George Rankin, Harry Potts, Tommy Eglington, Dave Hickson, Wally Fielding, Tommy Jones.

Southend United: Harry Threadgold, Bill Pavitt, Sandy Anderson, Frank Burns, Denis Howe, Jimmy Lawler, Joe Sibley, James Whyte, Roy Hollis, Kevin Baron, Ken Bainbridge.

SOUTHEND UNITED v. NORWICH CITY

20 August 1955   Football League Third Division (South)

Southend's first game back at Roots Hall for forty years was a perfect opening for a new era. The weather was very sunny and a huge crowd of 17,700 gathered to watch the spectacle. The players rose to the occasion and gave a great performance that lived long in the memory of those present. The Blues' football was swift and exciting and their fitness on a sweltering day was clearly evident. Southend fielded three debutants, Sam McCrory, Dickie Dowsett and John McGuigan and each gave a good account of himself.

Southend started well, despite facing the glaring sun, and were determined that the visitors would not get the honour of the first goal on the new ground. The first real opening fell to Dowsett who had received a fine ball from McCrory but his shot was smartly held by Nethercott in the Canaries' goal. Hollis and McGuigan had chances but both were fouled by McCrohan when about to shoot. Then Norwich took control for a period and Sammy Chung should have scored but his shot was intercepted by Doug Young and Bobby Brennan blazed the ball wide when well placed. Blues countered and McGuigan headed narrowly wide from a McCrory pass. Soon after, the same player look certain to score with another header but Ken Nethercott pulled off an amazing save to tip the ball over the bar.

Southend took a controversial lead after twenty-six minutes when Jim Duthie headed a corner towards goal and after a deflection Nethercott seemed to gather the ball only for Sammy McCrory to bundle the goalkeeper and the ball over the line. Despite the visitors' protestations the goal was allowed to stand. There were no more goals before half-time although Bill Lewis made a remarkable goal-line clearance to thwart Roy Hollis against his former club.

Southend dominated the second half with the sun behind them and captain Kevin Baron was an inspiration in midfield. The result of the game was secured with two goals in two minutes shortly after the restart. On fifty minutes great movement between Baron and McCrory allowed Roy Hollis to slam the ball into the corner of the net. The cheers for that goal had barely subsided when Dickie Dowsett danced into the penalty area and scored past Nethercott from an acute angle. Southend were all over the visitors although Norwich managed to reduce the arrears in the sixty-fourth minute when Reagan rounded Young and beat Harry Threadgold with a low drive.

Southend created numerous chances before the final whistle and Hollis really should have headed a fourth goal in the last minute but missed the target. Norwich managed to limit the damage to three goals with a mixture of good fortune, desperate defending and an inspired display from their goalkeeper, Ken Nethercott.

SOUTHEND UNITED 3

McCrory, Hollis, Dowsett

NORWICH CITY 1

Reagan

Above: Southend players greet the guests of honour at the opening of the new Roots Hall stadium.

Southend United: Harry Threadgold, Doug Young, Sandy Anderson, Jim Duthie, Dennis Howe, Jimmy Lawler, Dickie Dowsett, Sammy McCrory, Roy Hollis, Kevin Baron, John McGuigan.

Norwich City: Ken Nethercott, Maurice Norman, Bill Lewis, Roy McCrohan, Reg Foulkes, Ron Ashman, Peter Gordon, Sammy Chung, Ralph Hunt, Bobby Brennan, Martin Reagan.

COLCHESTER UNITED v. SOUTHEND UNITED

27 August 1955   Football League Third Division (South)

This was a spectacular local derby where the rampant Southend forwards cruelly exposed the weaknesses in the home side's rearguard. However, it was the home side that created the opening chance when Mike Grice's speculative lob from the flank nearly embarrassed Harry Threadgold. Southend broke downfield and Dennis Howe clipped the crossbar with a fierce drive with Percy Ames well beaten. However, The U's were grateful to their 'keeper when he kept out a barrage of shots from Baron, Dowsett and Hollis.

Ames was helpless to stop Southend taking the lead on forty minutes when a beautifully curling shot from Kevin Baron just curved in at the far post. Colchester were level within two minutes of the restart when Kevin McCurley scored with a low drive into the corner of Threadgold's net. However, Southend were stung into action and scored three times in the next seven minutes. Roy Hollis fired an unstoppable shot past Ames from the edge of the box. He scored again soon after when good work from Sammy McCrory carved out a chance for the prolific striker and he made no mistake from eight yards out. Hollis then turned provider when a deft flick played John McGuigan into a clear run on goal and the former St Mirren player slammed the ball past an overworked Ames to make the score 4-1.

On sixty-two minutes John Fowler scored for Colchester after some slack work at the back from Lawler and Duthie. Hollis completed his hat-trick on seventy-one minutes when another crisp, powerful shot gave Ames no chance to move. Seven minutes later Hollis scored the best goal of the game. He picked the ball up in the centre circle and strode forward. Huge gaps in the home defence opened up before him and he powered into the penalty area before crashing home his fourth goal of the afternoon. Colchester scored a last-minute penalty through McCurley after Fowler had been fouled by Lawler.

This was a brilliant performance by Southend who were clearly superior in every department. Their passing was accurate and devastating and the understanding between the players made the eleven Southend players a slick, goal-scoring machine.

COLCHESTER UNITED 3
  McCurley (2, 1 pen), Fowler

SOUTHEND UNITED 6
  Baron, Hollis (4), McGuigan

COLCHESTER UNITED *v.* SOUTHEND UNITED

Above left: Roy Hollis was the scourge of Colchester in this local derby at Layer Road.

Colchester United: Percy Ames, John Harrison, Benny Fenton, Bobby Hill, Billy Hunt, Bob Dale, Mike Grice, Sammy McLeod, Kevin McCurley, John Fowler, Peter Wright.

Southend United: Harry Threadgold, Doug Young, Sandy Anderson, Jim Duthie, Dennis Howe, Jimmy Lawler, Dickie Dowsett, Sammy McCrory, Roy Hollis, Kevin Baron, John McGuigan.

SOUTHEND UNITED v. MANCHESTER CITY

28 January 1956   FA Cup Fourth Round

Despite defeat, Southend United came away from this classic FA Cup-tie grabbing all the headlines alongside the famous visiting goalkeeper Bert Trautmann. It was a great credit to the club that the visitors had the fright of their lives in the Roots Hall mud but would eventually lift the trophy after a remarkable final against Birmingham City in which Trautmann kept goal for some of the game with a broken neck. The former German paratrooper, who seemed to be indestructible having been buried alive in a collapsed building during the Second World War as well as escaping from first a Russian and then a French Prisoner of War camp, always reckoned that his finest performance came in this fourth-round tie by the sea.

The weather in the Southend area had been horrendous and four days of heavy rain had reduced the newly laid and poorly drained Roots Hall pitch to a quagmire. Groundsman Sid Broomfield fought a losing battle with the pitch markings and despite continual repainting by hand the whitewash was scarcely visible. A small band of volunteers had helped sweep excess water off the pitch and rolled tonnes of building sand and crushed cockleshells into the swamp in an attempt to get the pitch in a playable condition. Referee Ernie Crawford arrived at the new ground and after a lengthy deliberation declared the pitch fit for play.

The rain returned with a vengeance just after one o'clock and the 2.45 p.m. start again looked in doubt. However, a large portion of the eventual record crowd of 29,500 was already in the ground and Crawford wisely stuck by his initial decision to play the game.

In reality the conditions were appalling; the *Sunday Pictorial* reporter Frank McGhee rated them 'the grimmest I have ever seen' and Ralph Hadley of the *People* compared the pitch to the trenches of Passchendaele. Both sides lined up in their change kits, the visitors, boasting four full internationals in their side, wore claret and blue and the Shrimpers sported an unusual all-old-gold strip.

Southend drove at the City defence from the off and were unlucky early on when Roy Hollis blazed wide when well placed. City took the lead on twenty-three minutes when on a rare attack their tiny winger Joe Hayes scooped in a soft shot that left Harry Threadgold rooted to the spot. The Shrimpers took the setback on the chin and fought back to create several good chances to equalise. The best chance came a minute before the break when Crichton Lockhart sent a cross over from the right wing. The cross deflected off David Ewing and was heading for the corner of the visitors' net. However, both United forwards, Hollis and Kevin Baron, watched in disbelief as Trautmann somehow stretched full length to tip the ball around the post for a corner kick.

The second half was scarcely underway when Dennis Howe played a lovely ball to Crichton Lockhart. He made light of the conditions, skilfully bringing the ball under control and charging towards Trautmann's net. Lockhart played Hollis in and the gangly forward ran through the puddles

SOUTHEND UNITED 0	MANCHESTER CITY 1
	Hayes

Sequence shot of Bert Trautmann's wonder save from Roy Hollis.

Southend United
Football Club Limited

SATURDAY, 28th JANUARY, 1956   KICK-OFF 2.45 p.m.

FOOTBALL ASSOCIATION CUP COMPETITION (4th Round)

SOUTHEND UNITED
VERSUS
MANCHESTER CITY

Photograph by C. W. Bruce   By kind permission of B.K.S. Charter Air Service

Next Home Match

SOUTHEND UNITED Res.

v

WATFORD Res.

Football Combination

S A T U R D A Y
4th F E B R U A R Y
KICK-OFF 3.0 p.m.

Nº 9992

Official Programme Price 3d.

SOUTHEND UNITED v. MANCHESTER CITY

to fire a perfect shot into the far corner – surely an equaliser for the Shrimpers! But the prolific striker hadn't met a 'keeper like Trautmann before and another tremendous save denied the home side.

The German was under siege from a barrage of Southend attacks and stopped everything the Shrimpers could throw at him, with Hollis being particularly unlucky. The Norfolk-born front man later described Trautmann as the greatest goalkeeper he had ever seen. Trautmann's greatest strength was his bravery and in one Southend attack a mass of mud and bodies confronted him as City desperately tried to clear the ball. Trautmann dived in among the flying boots and scooped the ball into his giant hands to relieve the pressure once again.

The German's most outstanding save came in the seventy-fourth minute when Lockhart again delivered a perfect cross for Hollis. The striker connected perfectly and at the last second managed to send the ball to the wrong side of the diving 'keeper. Hollis was certain he had scored this time but Trautmann somehow managed to change direction in mid-air and tip the ball over the crossbar. Despite a frantic final few minutes City survived and the match ended with a narrow victory to the visitors.

The whole match was played in a tremendous spirit, with referee Crawford recalling that he only blew for four fouls during the whole game and both teams received a well-deserved standing ovation at the end of the ninety pulsating minutes.

When asked about his amazing performance Trautmann, always a shy and modest man, said 'a goalkeeper can only look good against a good team'. City's captain Roy Paul, who won thirty-three Welsh caps, stated that 'we were very lucky, these Southend boys gave everything they had'.

Southend United: Harry Threadgold, Dennis Howe, Arthur Williamson, Jim Duthie, Jim Stirling, Jim Lawler, Crichton Lockhart, Sam McCrory, Roy Hollis, Kevin Baron, John McGuigan.

Manchester City: Bert Trautmann, Billy Leivers, Roy Little, Ken Barnes, David Ewing, Roy Paul, Billy Spurdle, Joe Hayes, Bobby Johnstone, Jack Dyson, Roy Clarke.

SOUTHEND UNITED v. LIVERPOOL

5 January 1957   FA Cup Third Round

Many people always associate Liverpool with being one of the country's top sides but in the mid-1950s they were a Second Division side, having been relegated in last place at the end of the 1953/54 season. However, this does not detract from an outstanding performance by the Shrimpers that earned a fourth-round home tie against Birmingham City. Trainer Wilf Dixon had produced a supremely fit team that not only out-muscled their visitors but overcame the notoriously heavy Roots Hall pitch.

Liverpool arrived at Roots Hall in confident mood with their goalkeeper, Tommy Younger, being ranked as one of the finest in Europe. The visitors kicked off and broke forward, and Billy Liddell drove the ball goalwards but Harry Threadgold gathered effortlessly. Southend's first effort came in the third minute when a dazzling run by Jim Duthie saw him beat four defenders before crashing the ball past the outstretched hand of Younger into the corner of the net. It was a truly brilliant goal and the much-vaunted visiting custodian had no chance of stopping his firm drive. Southend had their tails up following the early goal and Younger produced stunning saves from Jimmy Lawler and John McGuigan.

Another excellent chance came in the twenty-eighth minute when Sammy McCrory placed a lofted ball over the top of the Liverpool defence and Jimmy Thomson ran past Lawrie Hughes and nodded the ball forward. His left-foot shot bought another spectacular save from Younger. Roy Hollis also went close before half-time when Younger tipped his goal-bound shot out for a corner. But for the visiting goalkeeper the Blues could have ended the half four or five goals to the good. At the other end Harry Threadgold had a virtual spectator's role with only a header from Alan Arnell providing a testing moment.

Liverpool manager Phil Taylor, by all accounts, laid into his lacklustre troops at half-time and adjusted his tactics for the second period. It had the desired effect as in the opening minute after the restart a golden chance was carved open but Jimmy Melia missed an open goal. However, Liverpool were level in the forty-eighth minute when Liddell swung in a corner kick which was cleared by Jimmy Stirling. The ball fell to Geoff Twentyman some forty yards from goal. He belted the ball back into the penalty area and after several attempts by defenders to clear the ball John Wheeler lashed the loose ball home.

Liverpool were on top and Threadgold did well to cut out a centre from Arnell and then moments later denied A'Court from a close-range header. However, the home side weathered the storm and soon Southend launched a comeback. John McGuigan missed a great chance with the goal at his mercy. Southend then forced four consecutive corners and from the last of these a stinging shot from McGuigan hit the crossbar. Threadgold then kept Southend in the game with outstanding saves from

---

SOUTHEND UNITED 2   **LIVERPOOL 1**

Duthie, Thomson   Wheeler

Above right: Jimmy Thomson scored the winner against Liverpool.

Melia and A'Court, the latter when he shrugged off the threat of a serious injury by diving in the middle of flying boots.

The winning goal came in the eighty-second minute when McGuigan placed a perfect pass into the path of Jimmy Thomson. He shrugged off a tackle from Molyneux and calmly drove the ball under the body of a diving Younger in the visitor's goal. Roots Hall erupted with joy but the job was far from done. The Southend rearguard held firm under intense pressure. Four minutes from time A'Court nearly forced home a Liddell corner and two minutes later Liddell dribbled brilliantly into the penalty area. He was just about to shoot when Threadgold, again showing tremendous bravery, rushed out to block his effort. The whistle blew and a classic cup-tie giant-killing was secured thanks to a wonderful team effort.

Southend United: Harry Threadgold, Arthur Williamson, Sandy Anderson, Jim Duthie, Jimmy Stirling, Jimmy Lawler, Gordon Barker, Sam McCrory, Roy Hollis, Jimmy Thomson, John McGuigan.
Liverpool: Tommy Younger, John Molyneux, Ronnie Moran, Roy Saunders, Lawrie Hughes, Geoff Twentyman, Billy Liddell, John Wheeler, Alan Arnell, Jimmy Melia, Alan A'Court.

SOUTHEND UNITED v. QUEENS PARK RANGERS

31 August 1957   Football League Third Division (South)

Although this sensational performance by the Shrimpers was vociferously cheered by the Roots Hall faithful, the biggest ovation of the afternoon was handed to Queens Park Rangers goalkeeper Ron Springett. The future England international, nicknamed 'Spring-heel', turned in a magnificent performance which kept his woeful colleagues from total annihilation. Some of his breathtaking saves were incredible with the best being a full-stretch save to thwart a point-blank shot from John McGuigan. However, his heroics were wasted on his teammates, particularly his defence, which the home side carved open time and time again. Rangers' full-backs Pat Woods and Tony Ingham were given a particularly torrid time by Errol Crossan and John McGuigan.

It was a rampant period for the Blues as in the previous seven days they had won 5-0 at Exeter and defeated Norwich 5-2 at Roots Hall. Many of the 15,883 in attendance were still pouring into the ground when Sam McCrory opened the scoring on four minutes. Crossan's corner kick landed at the feet of Roy Hollis, he squared to McGuigan and his perfect chip was volleyed home by McCrory. Such was Southend's dominance in the opening period it was something of a surprise that it was thirty minutes before the second goal was scored. Rangers were a victim of their own offside trap when Duthie's accurate through ball found McCrory timing his run to perfection and the Irishman skilfully dribbled past Springett before slotting home.

Southend's possession play continued in the second half and Springett's brilliance kept out certain goals for McGuigan, Hollis and McCrory. However, the defence finally capitulated as the Blues knocked in four goals without reply in the closing thirteen minutes.

On seventy-seven minutes Duthie's inch-perfect free-kick allowed Hollis to head the ball past the despairing dive of the Rangers 'keeper. Four minutes later it was 4-0 when Crossan went on a brilliant twenty-yard run and with the Rangers defence backing off without a challenge, the Canadian feigned to pass to a colleague but then slammed in a low shot into the corner of the net from the edge of the box.

Three minutes from time another great left-footed drive from Crossan secured the fifth strike of the afternoon. Thirty seconds from time McGuigan made it a round half-dozen with a real opportunistic strike. He started the move with a long pass to Crossan, but Ingham intercepted the pass and played it to Woods. The full-back was slow in controlling the pass and McGuigan seized on his indecision and hit a right-foot shot into the net.

It was interesting to note that McGuigan, the left winger, had scored three goals in three games, two with his right foot, and Crossan the right-flank player scored two goals in this game with his 'weaker' left foot.

SOUTHEND UNITED 6   QUEENS PARK RANGERS 0
McCrory (2), Hollis, Crossan (2),
McGuigan

Above right: Errol Crossan, the Canadian-born outside right, netted twice against QPR.

Southend United: Harry Threadgold, Arthur Williamson, Dennis Howe, Jim Duthie, Jim Stirling, John Duffy, Errol Crossan, Sammy McCrory, Roy Hollis, Kevin Baron, John McGuigan.

Queens Park Rangers: Ron Springett, Pat Woods, Tony Ingham, George Petchey, Keith Rutter, Cecil Andrews, Arthur Longbottom, Bobby Cameron, Billy Finney, Eddie Smith, Peter Angell.

QUEENS PARK RANGERS v. SOUTHEND UNITED

11 January 1964   Football League Third Division

This was an amazing game, due largely to some erratic defending rather than goalscoring prowess. Manager Ted Fenton had tweaked his shot-shy forward line and at last found a combination that clicked, with right winger Derek Woodley in particularly devastating form.

It was Woodley that gave the vistors the lead on fourteen minutes. A swift interchange between Jimmy Conway and Ray Smith saw Smith tee the ball up for Woodley. His unstoppable twenty-five-yard shot left young Rangers goalkeeper Peter Springett with no chance. The home side levelled for the only time in the twenty-seventh minute when a moment's hesitation from Lou Costello saw Stuart Leary steal possession and square the ball to Brian Bedford, who rushed in at full tilt to beat Brian Rhodes in the Southend goal. The parity lasted only three minutes when the Blues took the lead again. Woodley's swirling cross was missed by Springett and Brian Taylor left the ball to go out for a goal kick. He didn't see John McKinven, who was able to stretch to cross the ball back brilliantly for an unmarked Conway who slid the ball into an unguarded net.

Rangers were in disarray and after thirty-two minutes Southend went 3-1 up when Costello took a short free-kick and found Woodley. He drove in a hard cross that zipped across the penalty box. Springett totally missed the speeding ball and in his haste to clear the danger Pat Brady sliced the ball into the net for a calamitous own goal.

The Hoops reduced the arrears on fifty-six minutes when the seventeen-year-old Greek winger Seth Vafiadis scored from a rebound after Rhodes pulled off a brilliant save to deny Bedford a second goal. The home players and spectators had erupted just prior to the second Rangers goal when loud appeals for a foul by Costello were waved away and moments after the goal George McLeod, their new signing from Brentford, was upended by the same player in the penalty area. Furious Rangers players surrounded the referee but their arguments for a spot kick were ignored.

To make tempers fray even further Southend scored again two minutes later. Terry Bradbury's lofted free-kick was superbly hooked into the roof of the net by Ray Smith to make it 4-2 to the visitors. Minutes later another penalty appeal was turned down when Tony Bentley was accused of handling the ball in breaking up another Rangers attack.

The proceedings did calm down but the temperature was rising again in the seventy-ninth minute when Rangers scored through Stuart Leary. It resulted from a rare error of judgement from Peter Watson, who thought McLeod's swerving cross was going wide but Leary rushed in to send a bullet header past Rhodes in the Southend goal. Southend secured the points in the eighty-sixth minute when Jimmy Conway scored the best goal of the game. Ray Smith's clever ball was flicked on by

QUEENS PARK RANGERS 4

Bedford, Vafiadis, Leary (2)

SOUTHEND UNITED 5

Woodley, Conway (2),
P. Brady (o.g.), Smith

Above right: Jimmy Conway scored two of Southend's five at Loftus Road.

Conway. His header took out Springett and after a smart sidestep left Andy Malcolm floundering, Conway slid the ball home for Southend's fifth of the afternoon.

The scoring was not done with and Rangers struck again in injury time when Leary outpaced Watson and scored with a rasping fifteen-yard drive which Rhodes could only help into the net.

Queens Park Rangers: Peter Springett, Brian Taylor, Pat Brady, Andy Malcolm, Ray Brady, Mike Keen, Seth Vafiadis, Brian Bedford, Stuart Leary, Malcolm Graham, George McLeod.

Southend United: Brian Rhodes, Lou Costello, Bobby King, Tony Bentley, Peter Watson, Terry Bradbury, Derek Woodley, Ray Smith, Jimmy Conway, Mike Beesley, John McKinven.

Brighton & Hove Albion v. Southend United

27 November 1965   Football League Division Three

A classic match due only to the ineptitude of the awful Southend defence that resulted in this record Football League defeat for the Shrimpers. Former player Alf Smirk, the *Southend Standard* reporter, called it 'United's Day of Soccer Shame'. 'Laughing stock' and 'The worst ever team' were two of the comments made from irate supporters in a savage attack on the club's management.

Southend fielded youngster Ray White in goal and although the shell-shocked 'keeper was at fault for some of the goals the defence in front of him offered no cover whatsoever. The forward line was equally inept with fully thirty-two minutes elapsing before a weak shot from Malcolm Slater registered a noteworthy effort on the home side's goal. The Albion were superior in every department and took the lead in the seventh minute when ex-Arsenal man Jimmy Magill whipped a long kick into the danger area. The ball was cleared but was met well by Jimmy Collins, and his six-yard drive found the net while three Blues defenders looked on helplessly. It was 2-0 after fifteen minutes when the hapless White could only help a John Goodchild corner into his own net. Seven minutes later it was three when a cross from Wally Gould sailed into the net without a challenge being made.

Amazingly the fourth goal did not arrive until the fifty-ninth minute but signalled the opening of the floodgates as the Seagulls scored three in four minutes. Jack Smith scored the fourth from close range after Southend had kicked two goal-bound shots off the line. He scored again two minutes later when he was allowed to run though unchallenged and shot home. A minute later White was slow to narrow the angles and Goodchild's shot found the net.

Southend then pulled one back when Mel Slack scored. He was the only Southend player that came out of the shambles with his head held high. The lone goal came after seventy-two minutes when he accepted a pass from Bradbury and hit a fierce shot from thirty yards which was in the back of the net before Bryan Powney had the chance to move. Minutes later Terry Bradbury hobbled off after a heavy challenge and his replacement, Bobby King, necessitated a reshuffle of the side, with Andy Smillie dropping back to wing half. The reshaped line-up lasted until the final five minutes when Albion scored three more goals to pile on the humiliation. In the eighty-fifth minute a lob from Baxter allowed Charlie Livesey to head home number seven.

Jack Smith completed his hat-trick in the eighty-eighth minute when he unleashed a bullet shot from twenty-five yards. The rout was completed in injury time when Collins' fine through ball found Livesey in acres of space. He controlled the ball and ran though a static defence to find the net with ease. 'We want ten' bellowed the home fans but time ran out and the humiliated Southend players sought the welcome sanctuary of the dressing room. This classic display of incompetence could have been worse as Brighton missed at least three certain goals. The season got no better as the Blues finished twenty-first in the table and were relegated for the first time in their League history.

BRIGHTON & HOVE ALBION 9   **SOUTHEND UNITED 1**
  Collins, Goodchild (2), Gould,   Slack
  Smith (3), Livesey (2)

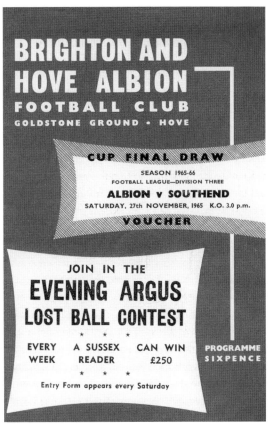

Above left: Mel Slack was the one Southend player to come out of this debacle with his reputation intact.

Brighton & Hove Albion: Bryan Powney, Jimmy Magill, Robert Baxter, Derek Leck, Norman Gall, David Turner, Wally Gould, Jimmy Collins, Charlie Livesey, Jack Smith, John Goodchild.

Southend United: Ray White, Tony Bentley, John Neal, Mel Slack, Eddie May, Terry Bradbury, Malcolm Slater, Chris Barnard, Derek Woodley, Andy Smillie, John McKinven. Sub: Bobby King (for Bradbury)

SOUTHEND UNITED v. KING'S LYNN

16 November 1968   FA Cup First Round

Veteran *Standard* columnist and former Shrimpers star Alf Smirk described this match as 'The Slaughter of the Innocents' and considering the Lynn goalkeeper stopped six certain goals and both Phil Chisnall and Gary Moore both had goals harshly disallowed, Smirk's analogy was not very far off the mark.

The Linnets started brightly when Micky Wright, making his 418th consecutive appearance, shot wide from a first-minute corner. The visitors' only other chance came in the twenty-second minute when Malcolm Lindsay headed over the bar from a well-placed free-kick. Apart from that it was a procession for the home side and the game was barely two minutes old when the visiting defence was breached for the first time. Chisnall intercepted a misplaced pass and set up Gary Moore, who drilled the ball past Norman Coe in the Lynn goal.

The game remained a contest until the twenty-sixth minute when Southend scored again. Chisnall was again the provider and his cross was netted by Billy Best but only after Coe made a brilliant save from his initial strike. Three minutes later it was 3-0 when some excellent work from Eddie Clayton resulted in a deep cross which Chisnall managed to net from a very acute angle. Six minutes before half-time and the Blues went 4-0 up when Chico Hamilton's long cross was headed into his own net by right-back Tony Haskins as he attempted to clear for a corner.

The fifth goal came in the sixty-second minute a few minutes after Moore had a goal disallowed for controlling the ball with his hands. The fifth went to Billy Best who stabbed home a Hamilton pass from close range. Best completed his hat-trick on seventy-two minutes when he finished a move he started after a swift interchange with Hamilton.

Southend scored three times in the last ten minutes as the visitors fell apart completely. The seventh goal went to Gary Moore who bundled the ball home after John Kurila flicked on a corner kick by Ian Hamilton. Haskins' poor afternoon was compounded in the eighty-first minute when his miscued clearance went straight to Phil Chisnall and his low drive arrowed into the corner of the beleaguered 'keeper's net. The rout was completed a minute from time when an excellent overlapping run from full-back Tony Bentley produced a pinpoint cross which allowed the powerful Gary Moore to outjump the defence and head into the corner of the net.

SOUTHEND UNITED 9   **KING'S LYNN 0**

  Moore (3), Best (3),
  Chisnall (2), Haskins (o.g.)

Above left: Phil Chisnall scored two of the Shrimpers' nine against King's Lynn.

Southend United: Trevor Roberts, Tony Bentley, Graham Birks, Sammy McMillan, Mickey Beesley, John Kurila, Eddie Clayton, Billy Best, Gary Moore, Phil Chisnall, Ian Hamilton. Sub: John Baber (not used)

King's Lynn: Coe, Haskins, Mullett, Brooks, Porter, Wright, Savino, Davies, Lindsay, Jenkins, Clarke. Sub: Hawksby (not used)

Southend United v. Brentwood Town

7 December 1968   FA Cup Second Round

Less than a month after the demolition of King's Lynn, Southend went one better as FA Cup history was created when Brentwood Town were put to the sword in an embarrassingly one-sided game at Roots Hall. Gary Moore and Billy Best, the Shrimpers' prolific strike force, had hit hat-tricks against King's Lynn and repeated the feat against the now-defunct Essex outfit. It is the only occasion in the long history of the competition that the same players have scored hat-tricks in consecutive rounds.

The Southend goal machine slipped into gear in the opening minute when Eddie Clayton held the ball up well on the left and played in Graham Birks on a superb overlapping run. His cross was spot-on and Gary Moore headed in at the far post. The visitors were briefly back in the game in the seventeenth minute when John Kurila's under strength back pass was intercepted by Reg Stratton who rounded Trevor Roberts to equalise. Parity only lasted three minutes when Moore elegantly headed in Ian Hamilton's accurate cross. The third goal arrived after thirty-five minutes when Sammy McMillan shot home smartly after an exquisite one-two with Billy Best. Moore completed his hat-trick on fifty-two minutes when he sent a flashing header past Billy Dunbar after Hamilton sent over another pinpoint centre. Eleven minutes later an identical combination saw Hamilton cross again for Moore to score with his fourth headed goal of the afternoon.

Billy Best then decided to get in on the act and promptly outshone his strike partner by scoring the remaining five goals, including four in the final six minutes! His first strike came after seventy-one minutes when Hamilton's curling corner deceived Dunbar and Best was on hand to head into an unguarded net. Goal number seven was scored in the eighty-fourth minute when Hamilton's cross, this time from the left flank, was again headed home by the former Northampton striker. Three minutes later Best, remarkably, completed another hat-trick of headed goals when he nipped in to nod the ball past Dunbar after Moore had flicked on

Almost directly from the kick-off Moore barged his way into the area and with the shattered Brentwood defence falling all around him, he squared for Best to slam home number nine. In injury time double figures were claimed when McMillan's perfect through ball allowed Best to cleverly clip the ball over the advancing goalkeeper to find the empty net.

The final whistle just denied the Blues beating their thirty-four-year-old club record, also set in the FA Cup, when Golders Green were beaten by the same score.

SOUTHEND UNITED 10
 Moore (4), McMillan,
 Best (5)

BRENTWOOD TOWN 1
 Stratton

Southend United: Trevor Roberts, Tony Bentley, Graham Birks, Sammy McMillan, Mickey Beesley, John Kurila, Eddie Clayton, Billy Best, Gary Moore, Phil Chisnall, Ian Hamilton. Sub: John Baber (not used)

Brentwood Town: Dunbar, Jones, Butterfield, Maynard, Loughton, Stevenson, Foster, Mansfield, Stratton, Dilsworth, Hyde. Sub: Bumpstead (for Mansfield)

TOUR TO RUSSIA

28 July to 5 August 1971

A ground-breaking tour behind the Iron Curtain saw Southend narrowly lose all four games in an arduous trip to Russia. The club made such an impact on their hosts that top outfit Zenit Leningrad were sent to Roots Hall for a friendly a year later as a thank-you for the visit.

The first game came in Kalinin, some 100 miles north-west of Moscow, in front of 19,000 spectators. The visitors were presented with bouquets of flowers before the kick-off, which they in turn passed on to spectators – a move that went down well with the host crowd who applauded warmly when Southend attacked.

Southend were forced to field a slightly weakened team as Gary Moore had not recovered from a virus, Bill Garner had an upset stomach and Brain Albeson had limped out of a training session with a strained ankle.

The game's only goal came after five minutes when some sloppy marking saw Kalinin's forward Mosalenkov score with ease past Southend's Australian goalkeeper John Roberts. Southend fared much better having reorganised the side at half-time but despite numerous attacks on the home goal an equaliser was not forthcoming.

The second match occurred two days later when the team arrived at Tula, some 100 miles south of the capital after a gruelling road journey. However, on arrival the club received news that their fourth scheduled game against Lokomotiv Moscow had been postponed due to fixture congestion and officials were hastily trying to find a last-minute replacement.

The Southend players watched Tula win a league game 5-1 that night and were more than a little apprehensive to hear that the local side contained three full internationals. Southend again opened the game uncertainly and went behind in the twelfth minute when Mishustin shot home as the defence failed to clear their lines. Southend levelled on thirty minutes when Terry Johnson netted the rebound after the home 'keeper could only parry a Bill Garner shot. Tula took the lead in the forty-seventh minute when Roberts was surprised by a dipping shot from full-back Mastrukov. Southend had several opportunities to level in the closing moments when they won a string of corners.

The third game came in the Black Sea resort of Sochi when 9,000 saw a team selected from local sides defeat the Blues by 2-0 with early goals, in the tenth and eleventh minutes, being the downfall of the tourists. The game was played in searing ninety-degree heat, a factor that led to Keith Lindsey breaking down in training. The game was spoilt somewhat in the second half when Bill Garner reacted to a robust tackle from a home defender and both men were sent off.

KALININ VOLGA 1	SOUTHEND UNITED 0
TULA METALLIST 2	SOUTHEND UNITED 1
BLACK SEA SELECT XI 2	SOUTHEND UNITED 0
SHINNIK JAROSAVL 1	SOUTHEND UNITED 0

Keith Lindsey collapsed in the extreme heat of Sochi on the banks of the Black Sea.

СТАДИОН ЯРОСЛАВСКОГО ОРДЕНА ЛЕНИНА И ОРДЕНА
ОКТЯБРЬСКОЙ РЕВОЛЮЦИИ ШИННОГО ЗАВОДА

МЕЖДУНАРОДНЫЙ
ТОВАРИЩЕСКИЙ МАТЧ

5 августа 1971 года
№ 12 (262)

ФУТБОЛ

„САУСЕНД ЮНАЙТЕД" — „ШИННИК"
Англия   СССР
Начало игры в 18 час. 30 мин.

The programme issued for the Shinnik Jasosavl match.

Another arduous 300-mile trip saw the club complete their obligations for a fourth game against late replacements Shinnik Jarosavl. Strangely, given the late organisation of this match, it was the only one that spawned a match programme. The match was another narrow defeat when Roberts and Lindsey misjudged the pace of a back pass due to the length of the grass and home forward Raigold nipped in to score the only goal of the game.

It was an eventful but tiring tour and chairman Bill Rubin commented, 'The hospitality was very good, particularly that of the ordinary supporters. They were all delighted to see us and will be happy for any English club to visit their country.'

Southend teams:

Against Kalinin Volga: John Roberts, Keith Lindsey, Alex Smith, Dave Elliott, John Piekalnetis, Joe Jacques, Terry Johnson, Billy Best, George Duck, Ray Ternent, Bernie Lewis.

Against Tula Metallist: John Roberts, Keith Lindsey, Alex Smith, Dave Elliott, Dave Barnett, Joe Jacques, Terry Johnson, Billy Best, Bill Garner, Ray Ternent, Peter Taylor.

Against the Black Sea Select XI: John Roberts, Alex Smith, Ray Ternent, Dave Elliott, Brian Albeson, Joe Jacques, Bernie Lewis, Peter Hunt, Bill Garner, Billy Best, Peter Taylor. Subs: Dave Barnett (for Elliott), Terry Johnson (for Taylor) and George Duck (for Lewis)

Against Shinnik Jarosavl: John Roberts, Keith Lindsey, Alex Smith, Dave Elliott, Brian Albeson, Joe Jacques, Terry Johnson, Billy Best, Bill Garner, George Duck, Ray Ternent. Sub: Peter Taylor (for Johnson)

SOUTHEND UNITED v. CAMBRIDGE UNITED

21 April 1972   Football League Fourth Division

Despite this defeat Southend remained in a good position for promotion. Their nearest rivals, Lincoln City, were held to a draw by Aldershot the following afternoon which all but ended their promotion hopes.

Southend's biggest ever Fourth Division gate of 17,059 packed into Roots Hall to watch this important Friday-night game. Southend dominated the opening exchanges and it looked only a matter of time before they opened the scoring. Only a couple of wonder saves from Peter Vasper stopped two certain goals for the prolific Billy Best. However, in the twenty-fifth minute tragedy struck when goalkeeper Derek Bellotti was stretchered off with a dislocated elbow. It was his first real test in the game when he rushed out to dispossess Brian Greenhalgh. He plucked the ball off the striker's foot but then landed awkwardly on a hard pitch. The silence that greeted his departure on a stretcher signalled that the Blues were up against it to secure the points needed for promotion. Young substitute Peter Taylor, all 5ft 7in of him, bravely donned the stricken goalkeeper's shirt and went between the sticks.

Despite the odds being stacked against the Blues they took the lead in the forty-seventh minute when Bill Garner drove home a neat pass from Billy Best. Then Ray Ternent hesitated when played through by Dave Elliott when a second goal looked certain. Ternent fluffed the chance and Vasper made an easy save.

Taylor did well in goal and made competent stops from Greenhalgh and David Lill. However, skipper Joe Jacques and Ray Ternent marshalled the backline well and protected the stand-in custodian. Cambridge struggled to break through and became increasingly frustrated. Jimmy Thompson and David Lill found their way into the referee's notebook as they lost their composure. However, in the seventy-second minute the Southend rearguard's keenness to protect their goalkeeper led to their downfall when Brian Albeson clattered into Taylor and Greenhalgh lashed home the loose ball. Albeson then made another error six minutes later when his weak headed clearance found Greenhalgh in space and he duly gave Cambridge the lead.

Manager Arthur Rowley gambled in the closing minutes by putting Alex Smith in goal, allowing Peter Taylor to try and grab a late equaliser but it was not to be. However, Southend managed to draw their last three games and finished second behind champions Grimsby Town. Lincoln City finished fifth, a point away from the promotion places.

SOUTHEND UNITED 1	CAMBRIDGE UNITED 2
Garner	Greenhalgh (2)

SOUTHEND UNITED *v.* CAMBRIDGE UNITED

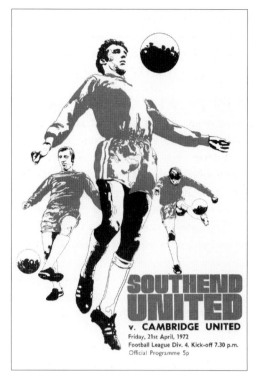

Above right: Derek Bellotti was stretchered off with a dislocated elbow.

Southend United: Derek Bellotti, Ray Ternent, Alex Smith, Dave Elliott, Brian Albeson, Joe Jacques, Terry Johnson, Billy Best, Bill Garner, Gary Moore, Dennis Booth. Sub: Peter Taylor (for Bellotti)

Cambridge United: Peter Vasper, Jimmy Thompson, Vic Akers, Alan Guild, Terry Eades, Dennis Walker, Ron Walton, Brian Greenhalgh, David Lill, Chris Foote, Bryan Conlon. Sub: Keith Pointer (not used)

Walsall v. Southend United

6 September 1975   Football League Third Division

A very exciting game saw Southend produce their first away win since November 1974 when Preston were defeated 4-1 at Deepdale. Striker Peter Silvester grabbed the headlines with a well-taken hat-trick but he was the first to admit that the points were won as the result of a tremendous team effort.

Southend took the lead with seventy-one seconds on the clock when Silvester turned well to fire home from a dangerous cross from young Ronnie Pountney. The lead was doubled in the ninth minute when the former Reading striker drove home from the edge of the box after Stuart Parker headed back a cross from Terry Nicholl.

The Southend side had to overcome a flag-happy linesman and a referee, Les Hayes, who made some strange decisions to say the least. In the thirty-seventh minute the official pointed to the penalty spot when Dave Cunningham seemed to make nothing more than a challenge for possession against Alan Buckley. Buckley seemed as surprised as anyone but gladly stroked home the spot kick. Walsall then unleashed a furious assault on the visitors' goal and a superb display from Malcolm Webster kept Southend from a barrage of goals. He twice denied Buckley and pulled off a wonder save from Miah Dennehy. However, Southend weathered the storm despite a below-par performance from Alan Moody and Neil Townsend looking short of match practice following a lengthy lay-off due to injury. Young Scot Dave Cunningham, preferred in midfield to Stuart Brace, also caused some concerns with some ill-advised back passes.

Southend responded to the pressure with the best possible answer by scoring a third goal in the fifty-eighth minute. Alan Little put a free-kick into the penalty area and a quick interchange between Townsend and Parker allowed Silvester to slam home for his hat-trick goal. Walsall's heads seemed to go down at this point and even though Miah Dennehy scored in the eighty-third minute with a crisp shot, the Saddlers rarely threatened in the closing stages. However, Peter Silvester was left with only the memory of his second career hat-trick as the home side refused to give him the match ball as a memento of his clinical hat-trick. Silvester said, 'It wasn't offered and it seemed to be a bit of a cheek to ask for it. Still I'm not worried, the important thing is that we are back on the winning trail.'

WALSALL 2   **SOUTHEND UNITED 3**

Buckley (pen), Dennehy   Silvester (3)

Above left: Hat-trick hero Peter Silvester.

Walsall: Mick Kearns, Roger Fry, Colin Harrison, Dave Robinson, John Saunders, Nick Atthey, Miah Dennehy, George Andrews, Bernie Wright, Alan Buckley, Alan Birch. Sub: Terry Spinner (for Atthey)

Southend United: Malcolm Webster, Dave Worthington, Tony Taylor, Alan Little, Neil Townsend, Alan Moody, Terry Nicholl, Ronnie Pountney, Stuart Parker, Dave Cunningham, Peter Silvester. Sub: Andy Ford (not used)

Southend United v. Liverpool

10 January 1979   FA Cup Third Round

This was a famous night when Southend gave the two-time European champions Liverpool a mighty fright in front of a record gate of 31,033 at Roots Hall. The match had originally been postponed on the previous Saturday when, despite a herculean effort to clear snow and ice from the pitch, it was decided in the interests of public safety that the terraces were still too icy and the game was rescheduled for the following Wednesday. Southend had earned the dream tie having disposed of Peterborough United and Watford in the opening rounds.

Southend manager Dave Smith spent the days leading up to the match talking up his side's chances, stating, 'I am getting fed up telling people we've got players of quality at this club.' He revealed that his pre-match team talk focused on the fact that his players would surprise themselves. Of course, the wily old fox was right and his troops were more than a match for their lauded opponents.

Conditions were still treacherous when the match kicked off with fans still trying to get into the ground. Southend seemed the more sure-footed and skipper Alan Moody and centre-back partner Tony Hadley were faultless as they snuffed out the threat of David Fairclough and Kenny Dalglish. Goalkeeper Mervyn Cawston was only tested on a few occasions, firstly when Fairclough broke free from his marker but as he was about to shoot Cawston slid out to whip the ball off his feet. Later Cawston tipped over a clever lob from Emlyn Hughes and then saved a point-blank header from Alan Hansen from the resulting corner.

Not that it was all one-way traffic. In fact, the home side enjoyed the majority of possession. Twenty-year-old Phil Dudley was magnificent in midfield and Ronnie Pountney gained much praise for his man-marking job on the dangerous Ray Kennedy. Southend's best chance came in the forty-second minute when a super through ball from Gerry Fell found Derrick Parker in space and as he rushed through a goal looked certain. However, Ray Clemence showed the quality that earned so many England caps, and broke Southend hearts with a brave and incredible save.

In the second half the temperature dropped and the pitch got even harder but Southend still took the game to Liverpool. In the eightieth minute the home crowd bayed for a penalty when Parker went down in the penalty area under a challenge from Phil Neal and Alan Hansen. However, TV replays proved undoubtedly that the conditions were responsible for Parker losing his footing, rather than a trailing leg, and Keith Hackett's decision was proven to be correct.

The ball was breaking sharply on the frosty pitch and Liverpool were more than happy to shut up shop and take the tie back to Anfield the following Monday. Liverpool boss Bob Paisley was rarely known to comment on his side's opponents but offered praise for Southend by saying, 'They fought tremendously hard and deserve next week's trip to our place.'

SOUTHEND UNITED 0   **LIVERPOOL 0**

SOUTHEND UNITED v. LIVERPOOL

Above: Derrick Parker wasted a glorious chance to sink the champions of Europe.

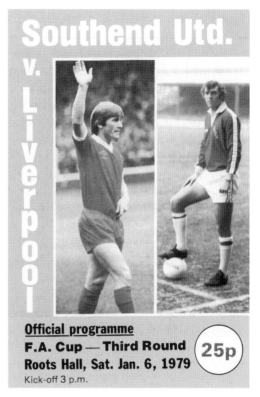

Southend Utd.

v.

Liverpool

Official programme
F.A. Cup — Third Round
Roots Hall, Sat. Jan. 6, 1979
Kick-off 3 p.m.

25p

Southend earned the lion's share of record Roots Hall receipts of £36,559 and a healthy cut from the replay at Anfield, which Liverpool won 3-0. However, the ultimate defeat didn't hide the tremendous achievement in the home game. Typical headlines in the national press were 'Southend Scare Europe Giants' and 'Southend Put Paisley Boys On the Rack'.

Southend United: Mervyn Cawston, Micky Stead, Steve Yates, Micky Laverick, Tony Hadley, Alan Moody, Colin Morris, Ronnie Pountney, Derrick Parker, Phil Dudley, Gerry Fell. Sub: John Walker (for Fell)
Liverpool: Ray Clemence, Phil Neal, Emlyn Hughes, Phil Thompson, Ray Kennedy, Alan Hansen, Kenny Dalglish, Jimmy Case, David Fairclough, Terry McDermott, Graeme Souness. Sub: Steve Heighway (for McDermott)

BOLTON WANDERERS v. SOUTHEND UNITED

28 August 1979   Football League Cup Second Round, First Leg

This was the first time Southend had been victorious against top-flight opposition on their own ground. What made the result all the more creditable was that Southend were playing with ten men for more than an hour.

The referee, Michael Peck of Doncaster, was a central figure in the game and seemed to many supporters to judge tackles differently depending on which team was the aggressor. In the opening minute Bolton midfielder Len Cantello clattered into Colin Morris, who required lengthy treatment, but was let off with a mild admonishment. Roy Greaves and Peter Nicholson also made some ugly-looking challenges but went unpunished. Yet every time the Blues made a tackle the result was at best a severe talking to and more often a yellow card was brandished.

One yellow card was waved in the direction of Dave Cusack in the fourteenth minute when he flattened the veteran former Manchester United forward Alan Gowling. It was a warranted booking but in the thirty-fourth minute Cusack won the ball fairly from Neil Whatmore but was inexplicably shown a second yellow card and sent packing down the tunnel.

The Blues managed to get to half-time with their goal intact and manager Dave Smith reshuffled his pack during the interval, bringing Tony Hadley back into the rearguard. The reorganisation would work but not before the First Division outfit took the lead in the fifty-first minute. Some clever work down the right from Neil McNab resulted in a pinpoint cross that Gowling gratefully nodded in from close range. However, the Trotters' lead lasted just three minutes – and what a wonderful equaliser it was. Tony Hadley played a great defence-splitting ball fully fifty yards straight to the feet of Colin Morris. The little midfielder took the ball in his stride and while Bolton 'keeper Jim McDonagh rushed out to narrow the angle Morris clipped the ball deftly into the corner of the net.

Southend took an unlikely lead in the sixty-third minute when another great ball from Hadley was flicked on by Micky Tuohy. Morris outpaced Roy Greaves and shot home his second goal of the game.

Southend had to contend with a real battery of attacks in the final twenty minutes but the defence held firm. In goalkeeper Mervyn Cawston the Blues had a custodian at the top of his form and he stopped everything that was thrown at him. In the last minute Cawston pulled off a save that bought comparisons to Gordon Banks' famous save against Pele. Whatmore's header seemed certain to draw the scores level but Cawston somehow dived full length to scoop the ball to safety.

The final whistle blew and the ten brave Southend players had overcome tremendous adversity. They rejoined their distraught colleague Cusack in the dressing room, where he admitted to a mixed

BOLTON WANDERERS 1	SOUTHEND UNITED 2
Gowling	Morris (2)

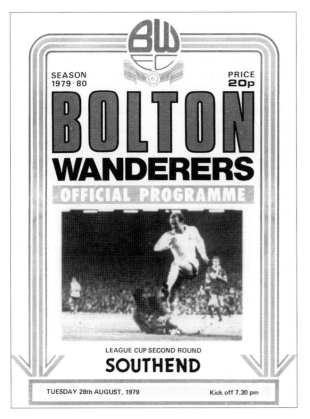

Above right: Midfielder Colin Morris turned in a match-winning performance.

sense of shame for his first-ever dismissal but huge relief and pride in the performance of his teammates.

The second leg at Roots Hall ended goal-less and earned Southend an epic three-game match against local rivals West Ham United.

Bolton Wanderers: Jim McDonagh, Dave Clement, Peter Nicholson, Roy Greaves, Paul Jones, Mike Walsh, Tadeusz Nowak, Neil Whatmore, Alan Gowling, Len Cantello, Neil McNab. Sub: Willie Morgan (for Nowak)

Southend United: Mervyn Cawston, Phil Dudley, Alan Moody, Dave Cusack, Steve Yates, Micky Stead, Tony Hadley, Anton Otulakowski, Micky Tuohy, Derrick Parker, Colin Morris. Sub: Ronnie Pountney (for Otulakowski)

Burnley v. Southend United

A brilliant result for Southend, who were enjoying a great season back in the Third Division having won the Fourth Division title the previous season. It was a tough-looking fixture with Burnley being on a run of only one defeat in their previous thirty-one matches at Turf Moor and challenging for the title, while the Blues were on the fringes of the promotion picture. Even more remarkable was the additional statistic that the Clarets had only conceded three goals in their previous nine home games.

It took the visitors only seven minutes to get the scoring underway when Derek Spence volleyed home from close range following a neat cross from Anton Otulakowski. Four minutes later it was 2-0 when Steve Phillips, recently signed from Northampton Town for £15,000, lashed in a fierce shot from the edge of the penalty box.

Having cantered into a comfortable lead, the match looked to be turning against the visitors in a crazy spell in the fifteen minutes leading up to the break. On thirty minutes some incredibly sloppy defending allowed Paul McGee to reduce the arrears. Then came a highly controversial moment which incensed the Southend players. The linesman raised his flag when Southend's rearguard moved out together to catch three Burnley attackers clearly offside. The flag then went down almost immediately and confused referee Bert Newsome waved play on, allowing future England international Trevor Steven to score with ease. Blues protested vehemently but the goal was allowed to stand. Moments later the referee compounded matters by sending off Southend centre-back Dave Cusack. He had been harshly cautioned earlier for a challenge on Billy Hamilton. Burnley right-back Brian Laws attacked the Southend area and Cusack looked to have made a superb saving tackle. However, he picked himself up to find referee Newsome waving first a yellow and then a red card at him. Nonetheless, manager Dave Smith earned his wages at half-time by galvanising his ten men to an almost unbelievable fightback.

With just three minutes gone in the second half Southend regained the lead when Spence headed home his second of the match. It was the goal that injected new life into the side and they promptly scored two more in the next nine minutes. In the fifty-first minute Paul Dixon upended Anton Otulakowski in the penalty area and Steve Phillips slotted home the spot kick. Garry Nelson, playing in midfield, made it 5-2 on the hour when Spence flicked on an Otulakowski corner allowing Nelson to bundle the ball past Alan Stevenson. Burnley then got another lucky break in the seventy-first minute when Steven's cross was turned into his own net by the otherwise faultless Otulakowski. The last twenty minutes ebbed and flowed from one end to another, Southend's defence were magnificent, tackling everything that moved while Phillips, Otulakowski and Pennyfather all missed easy chances to increase the lead.

BURNLEY 3

McGee, Steven,
Otulakowski (o.g.)

SOUTHEND UNITED 5

Spence (2), Phillips (2, 1 pen),
Nelson

Above: Northern Ireland international Derek Spence scored twice at Turf Moor.

The final whistle blew and an exhausted Blues team returned to the dressing room victorious. Veteran manager Dave Smith offered his opinion on the proceedings by saying 'Unbelievable, magnificent. There aren't really words adequate enough to describe how we performed out there tonight. Who would bet against us going up?'

Typically Southend faltered on the home straight, finishing seventh, while Burnley won the championship on goal difference from Carlisle United. Burnley's title was won at Roots Hall on the final day of the season when they triumphed 4-1, just twenty-four days after this amazing encounter at Turf Moor.

Burnley: Alan Stevenson, Brian Laws, Andy Wharton, Derek Scott, Paul Dixon, David Holt, Martin Dobson, Trevor Steven, Billy Hamilton, Paul McGee, Kevin Young. Sub: Phil Cavener (for Wharton)

Southend United: Mervyn Cawston, Micky Stead, Steve Yates, Ronnie Pountney, Alan Moody, Dave Cusack, Garry Nelson, Steve Phillips, Derek Spence, Glenn Pennyfather, Anton Otulakowski. Sub: Danny Greaves (not used)

Scunthorpe United v. Southend United

30 September 1983   Football League Third Division

This match represents the club's record away victory in a Football League match. What was even more remarkable is that it came in a relegation season when only two away wins were forthcoming, with the second happening in April at Lincoln City. Manager Peter Morris had been handed the reins at a late stage and his lack of preparation time saw a disjointed side finish twenty-second in the table, five points from safety. Morris' tenure in charge would end in dismissal in February.

The match at the Old Show Ground saw an injury-ravaged Scunthorpe side take the field sporting two young debutants and five teenagers, but the Irons had only conceded one goal in their previous three home games. However, the majority of the 3,335 crowd saw their side systematically dismantled by a rampant Blues team. Hero of the day was transfer-listed striker Steve Phillips, who grabbed a hat-trick, the fourth of his career. He was at loggerheads with manager Peter Morris having been dropped earlier in the season. He could not have signed off for a two-game suspension, having been sent off against Millwall at Roots Hall, in finer style.

The game was only forty-eight seconds old when Steve Collins swung in a corner, Greig Shepherd flicked on at the near post and Phillips crashed home an unstoppable volley. The Blues were supremely dominant in midfield with the energy of Glenn Pennyfather and newcomer Brian Ferguson being complemented by the subtlety of the veteran Billy Kellock. Their prompting created a catalogue of openings and in truth Southend really should have had more than the six they finally finished with.

The second came in the twenty-sixth minute when some clever play by Brian Ferguson saw him square the ball to Glenn Pennyfather and the blond midfielder lashed the ball in from twenty yards. Minutes into the second half something of rarity happened when full-back Micky Stead added the third goal. The veteran defender had not scored for three seasons when he picked the ball up in his own half. He advanced unchallenged and fired in a full-blooded shot from fully forty yards, giving the helpless Joe Neenan no chance in the home goal.

The fourth goal arrived after fifty-seventh minutes when some clever play down the flank saw an excellent cross from Pennyfather. Steve Phillips ran into space and headed home from an unmarked position. He completed his hat-trick a minute later when another well-placed drive found the back of Scunthorpe's net for the fifth goal of the game.

The sixth came in the sixty-ninth minute when Phillips' strike partner Greig Shepherd got a well-deserved goal. He picked up a smart through ball from Kellock and drove into the penalty area, leaving Les Hunter for dead before burying the ball past Neenan.

Strangely, at six goals down Scunthorpe had their best spell of the match, and despite their huge lead Southend were rattled and two rash challenges earned bookings for Pennyfather and Paul

---

SCUNTHORPE UNITED 1

Holden (pen)

SOUTHEND UNITED 6

Phillips (3), Pennyfather, Stead, Shepherd

SCUNTHORPE UNITED *v.* SOUTHEND UNITED

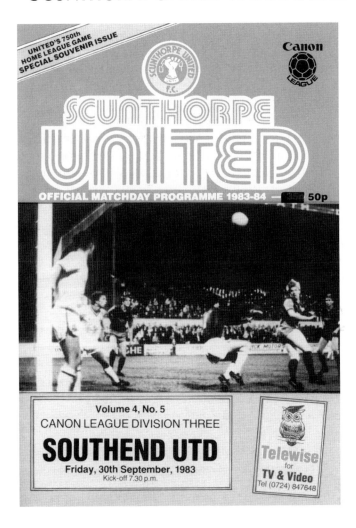

Clark. The home side pulled one back in the seventy-fourth minute when they won a penalty after Stead needlessly handled a Neil Pointon cross. Robbie Holden took the kick and gave on-loan custodian Gerry Peyton no chance from twelve yards.

Southend had more chances in the closing stages, notably when Hunter saved his side from further embarrassment when he made a goal-line clearance to deny centre-back Steve Yates a certain goal.

Scunthorpe United: Joe Neenan, Russell Richardson, Neil Pointon, Mike Brolly, John Green, Les Hunter, Paul O'Berg, Robbie Holden, Simon Snow, Mike Lester, David Hill. Sub: Tommy Graham (not used)

Southend United: Gerry Peyton, Micky Stead, Steve Collins, Glenn Pennyfather, Steve Yates, Paul Clark, Brian Ferguson, Billy Kellock, Roy McDonough, Greig Shepherd, Steve Phillips. Sub: Glen Skivington (not used)

SOUTHEND UNITED V. TORQUAY UNITED

11 May 1985   Football League Fourth Division

This was a vital game in the history of the club, one which in terms of skill would not rate as a classic match, but the sheer tension-filled minutes before Southend secured their Fourth Division status would stay with the 1,704 watching the game forever.

The Shrimpers had, in truth, performed abysmally in this their darkest season. The club were financially stricken under the controversial chairmanship of Anton Johnson and manager Bobby Moore, England's World Cup-winning captain, proved beyond doubt that a great player does not necessarily make a good manager. He had assembled arguably the worst squad ever to represent the club.

Southend's survival came down to the last day; only a win would suffice for them to avoid the ignominy of the re-election vote. The end-of-season lottery would pit the bottom four in the basement division against hopeful aspirants from the Conference. Clubs would petition their fellow clubs and, if a League club secured fewer votes than the Conference outfit, then they would be demoted. Southend would certainly have struggled as the cartel of northern-based clubs would have voted for each other. All this would actually become academic as on this occasion no applicant was forthcoming from the non-league scene. However, as Southend faced Torquay in the last game the club were not to know this and everything rested on the final ninety minutes of an awful campaign.

The match itself was a turgid affair with the visitors themselves firmly rooted to the foot of the table. Southend did not threaten Kenny Allen's goal until the forty-fourth minute when winger Alan Rogers drove into the penalty area from the left flank. The Gulls' right-back Derek Dawkins upended the former Plymouth player just inside the box and the referee awarded the Blues a desperately needed penalty kick. The all-important kick was handed to top scorer Steve Phillips, who had been dropped at Mansfield the previous week and was contemplating his future away from the club. The crowd favourite struck the kick well and the shot clipped the inside post and rolled along the line before nestling in the net. It was his twenty-third goal of the campaign and brought a huge sigh of relief from the Blues faithful. The second half saw Southend have the majority of possession and Phillips might have had a hat-trick, but twice contrived to hit the bar when well placed. Torquay's veteran goalkeeper Kenny Allen also played well and kept out decent shots from Warren May and Lil Fuccillo. Torquay's only real chance came nine minutes from time when a rare corner saw future Blues striker Mario Walsh trouble Jim Stannard in the home goal with a well-placed header.

The time wound down slowly but eventually the final whistle sounded and Southend were safe on goal difference, ahead of Halifax Town. The meagre crowd flooded onto the pitch and danced

SOUTHEND UNITED 1   **TORQUAY UNITED 0**
  Phillips (pen)

Above left: Beleaguered Southend manager Bobby Moore.

with delight that the points had been secured. This was a very poor Southend side with a creaky defence and no midfield creativity, and Phillips represented the only real goal threat. But the team had dug out a result when the pressure was on and manager Bobby Moore stated, 'If those supporters can take such pleasure from us keeping out of the bottom four then we must be optimistic for the future.'

Southend United: Jim Stannard, Micky Stead, Glenn Pennyfather, Paul Clark, Shane Westley, Steve Hatter, Lil Fuccillo, Ronnie Pountney, Warren May, Steve Phillips, Alan Rogers. Sub: Micky Engwell (not used)
Torquay United: Kenny Allen, Derek Dawkins, Derek Hall, Eddie Kelly, Derek Fowler, John Impey, Jon Durham, Micky Perry, Mario Walsh, Mark Loram, Steve Pugh. Sub: Andy O'Dell (for Walsh)

STOCKPORT COUNTY v. SOUTHEND UNITED

8 May 1987   Football League Fourth Division

Southend's stormy 1986/87 season, which had seen boss Dave Webb walk out after one too many disputes with chairman Vic Jobson back in March, hung on the final game of the season. A win at Stockport County's Edgeley Park would see the Blues, under the management of twenty-nine-year-old player Paul Clark, promoted to the Third Division. Anything else would allow Wolverhampton Wanderers in to grab the third automatic promotion slot. The Midlands club had won eleven out of their last dozen matches, with their only defeat coming, famously, to a Martin Ling header at Roots Hall. A Friday-night fixture at Stockport meant that three points for the Shrimpers would render Wolves' home match against lowly Hartlepool meaningless the following afternoon.

Southend United's noisy contingent of travelling fans were allocated half the Railway End terrace, which was in the process of being rebuilt. For a May evening the pitch was very muddy with large grassless patches in the centre circle and both penalty areas. Southend went into the game as favourites as Stockport had struggled at the wrong end of the table for the whole campaign under the management of future Southend boss Colin Murphy.

Southend took the initiative and after three minutes Glenn Pennyfather released Dave Martin on the right flank and his deep cross found Roy McDonough who could only head over Chris Marples' crossbar. After six minutes Paul Clark's raking free-kick again found McDonough, but once again his header was ineffective and was easily dealt with by Marples in the County goal. Blues continued to press and deservedly took the lead after ten minutes. Andy Rogers took a corner on the right side and Shane Westley rose high to head the ball forward. Dave Martin neatly flicked the ball up, allowing Glenn Pennyfather to volley home crisply from ten yards.

Stockport continued to employ the offside trap and McDonough, Cadette and Rogers were flagged on numerous occasions. The home side had their first chance on fourteen minutes when Andy Hodkinson's snap shot deflected off Westley for a corner. Two minutes later, Hodkinson's cross was headed out weakly by Westley and the loose ball fell to Levi Edwards who shot narrowly past Jim Stannard's left-hand post. Three minutes later County players and supporters unsuccessfully appealed for a penalty following Westley's clumsy challenge on Mark Sertori. The match then went into a prolonged period of poor play with neither midfield managing to assume control of the match.

On the half-hour mark, Pennyfather cleverly carved himself an opening following a good run but his shot was less impressive, slicing badly wide of the County net. On thirty-five minutes a sustained County attack saw Sertori head goalwards but Paul Clark was able to hack the ball away. The ball came straight back but Stannard gathered before getting injured following a very late and heavy challenge by Sertori. Three minutes later County skipper Trevor Matthewson gave a needless

---

STOCKPORT COUNTY 0   **SOUTHEND UNITED 2**

Pennyfather, Cadette

SEASON 1986-87

THE TODAY LEAGUE

DIVISION 4

VERSUS

SOUTHEND UNITED

Friday, 8th May 1987

Kick-off: 7.30 p.m.

Tonight's Match Sponsors are . . .

MSS (North West) Ltd. The Metal Professionals

Official Programme 50p

Stockport County v. Southend United

Southend players celebrate promotion at Stockport.

free-kick away following a blatant handball. Dave Martin took charge of the set piece and hit a terrific shot narrowly past the post.

County nearly levelled two minutes before the break when Martin's weak header found Les Robinson in space and his cross was flicked on by veteran striker Ernie Moss. Sertori latched onto the loose ball and his effort was superbly saved by Stannard to preserve the narrow lead. Moments later Southend won a free-kick and Derek Hall's accurate cross found Dave Martin unmarked but the former Wimbledon man could only head wide with Marples completely stranded.

As the condition of the pitch deteriorated, the match degenerated into a dour midfield battle. On fifty-seven minutes McDonough volleyed wide after good work from Hall and Rogers. County then turned the screw and Stannard produced a string of unbelievable saves to keep the Blues afloat. From a weak back pass from Martin the big 'keeper denied Phil Brown when clean though on goal. Then Ernie Moss fired in a rocket from twelve yards and Stannard managed to somehow tip the ball around the post for a corner.

After sixty-nine minutes Richard Cadette capitalised on an error in judgement by Ian McKenzie, who lost the bounce of the ball on the muddy surface, and the little striker sped goalwards. However, he then seemed to be in two minds whether to shoot or play in the unmarked McDonough. In the event he did neither and the chance was gone.

Cadette redeemed himself in the seventy-fourth minute when Southend won a corner. The corner was vehemently disputed by Hodkinson who perhaps justifiably claimed that Rogers had made the final contact. However, a short corner saw Hall play the ball to Rogers and his pacy cross allowed an unmarked Cadette to volley home right-footed from very close range. He ran to the massed ranks of Southend supporters to celebrate his thirty-first goal of a prolific campaign.

Southend finished strongly, having now broken the County spirit, with O'Shea and Cadette both squandering good opportunities.

A sizeable amount of Wolves supporters had swelled the home end but they traipsed out forlornly before the final whistle having been consigned to the lottery of the play-offs, which would eventually be won by Aldershot.

Southend wound down the clock and mercifully after just two minutes of injury time Southend's heroes were able to celebrate with their delirious supporters. The players threw their yellow shirts over the security fence to thank the travelling masses.

After the final whistle player-manager Paul Clark hailed the travelling support saying 'they follow us to the ends of the earth but turn up every week even when we haven't played very well, they are magnificent and a credit to the club.'

Stockport County: Chris Marples, Clive Evans, Ian McKenzie, Levi Edwards, Trevor Matthewson, Wayne Stokes, Andy Hodkinson, Ernie Moss, Mark Sertori, Les Robinson, Phil Brown. Sub: Billy Williams (not used)

Southend United: Jim Stannard, Dave Martin, Peter Johnson, Danny O'Shea, Shane Westley, Derek Hall, Paul Clark, Glenn Pennyfather, Richard Cadette, Roy McDonough, Andy Rogers. Sub: Dean Neal (not used)

Southend United v. Derby County

Southend's victory in this game was a truly remarkable achievement considering the club's abject form in the League under new manager Dick Bate. The club were on a run of six straight League defeats including heavy defeats at Gillingham (1-8), Notts County (2-6) and Port Vale (1-4). Indeed, the club's only victory of the season to that point had been a 4-2 triumph over Brentford in the first round second leg of the Littlewoods Cup, which was just sufficient to overturn a 2-1 deficit from the first leg.

So miserable were Bate's efforts to galvanise his team that he was relieved of his duties on the morning of Derby's visit to Roots Hall, with Southend player Paul Clark, then only twenty-nine, put in charge for a second spell. The First Division side boasted three England players: Mark Wright, John Gregory and legendary goalkeeper Peter Shilton, as well as Welsh international Geraint Williams.

Poor old Clark must have thought that everything was conspiring against him when at five o'clock a water main at Roots Hall burst, flooding the dressing rooms and leaving the ground without running water. A postponement looked inevitable but surprisingly, Derby manager Arthur Cox and the match referee, David Elleray, agreed to use the facilities on offer at the nearby Access Sports Club on Eastern Avenue.

It turned out to be a remarkable evening for the club as the defence with the worst goals-conceded record in the country held firm against the onslaught of the mighty Rams. Southend could have taken the lead as early as the seventh minute when a Roy McDonough flick-on released Lee Nogan, an eighteen-year-old striker on loan from Oxford United, but with Shilton beaten the youngster watched in dismay as his effort hit the post and was hooked away by Mark Wright. However, Southend did score in the twenty-eighth minute when Derby conceded a penalty after Ross McLaren inexplicably handled the ball in his own area. Maverick striker Roy McDonough stepped up and crashed the ball into the bottom corner, sending the England goalkeeper the wrong way. Southend had to defend for long periods but both Ling and McDonough squandered opportunities to increase the lead before half-time.

The second half continued with Southend's previously shaky defence holding out against a barrage of Derby attacks. The closest the visitors came to drawing level came on sixty-five minutes when John Gregory rattled Eric Steele's crossbar.

The match turned fully in Southend's favour in the seventy-first minute when Derby's striker, Bobby Davison, was dismissed for persistent arguing. Derby's ten men were unable to find an equaliser and Southend secured only their second ever triumph against top-flight opposition.

Paul Clark was rewarded with the player-manager's job, despite his relative youth, although it was his deflection that put Southend out of the competition in the next round when Graham Harbey's free-kick hit Clark before wrong-footing Eric Steele in a 0-1 defeat at Ipswich Town.

SOUTHEND UNITED 1   **DERBY COUNTY 0**

McDonough (pen)

SOUTHEND UNITED v. DERBY COUNTY

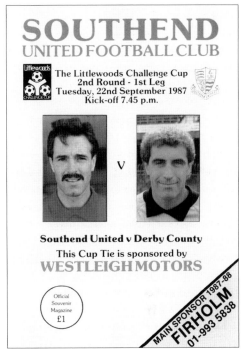

Above left: Roy McDonough held his nerve to beat England goalkeeper Peter Shilton with a penalty kick.

Southend United: Eric Steele, David Martin, Peter Johnson, Adrian Burrows, Shane Westley, Derek Hall, Martin Robinson, Glenn Pennyfather, Lee Nogan, Roy McDonough, Martin Ling. Subs: Paul Clark and Nicky Smith (not used)

Derby County: Peter Shilton, Paul Blades, Mike Forsyth, Geraint Williams, Mark Wright, Ross McLaren, Mel Sage, Phil Gee, Bobby Davison, John Gregory, Nigel Callaghan. Subs: Andy Garner (for Gee) and David Penney (not used)

ALDERSHOT *v.* SOUTHEND UNITED

9 September 1989   Football League Fourth Division

Southend enjoyed some high-scoring victories against Aldershot in the late 1980s and early 1990s but this away game at the Recreation Ground saw a scintillating performance by Dave Webb's troops, none more so than transfer-listed winger Gary Bennett. The former Chester City player gave left-back Ian Phillips a torrid time and opened the scoring in this rout of the Hampshire outfit.

The opening goal came after twelve minutes when a long throw-in from Paul Roberts was flicked on by gangly frontman Mario Walsh. His header found Bennett unmarked and he lashed the ball past David Coles from ten yards. Six minutes later another devastating move saw Mario Walsh cut the ball back for Martin Ling to score a certain goal. However, full-back Kevan Brown beat him to the cross and deftly guided the ball into the corner of his own net.

Aldershot were frankly outclassed in every department; in particular Peter Butler and Jason Cook dominated the midfield and reduced the home side to only sporadic attacks. The remainder of the half and the opening period of the second half saw the vistors peppering the home goal at will with Crown, Bennett, Walsh and Ling all guilty of profligacy in front of goal. It was therefore more than a little perplexing that Southend had to wait until the sixty-third minute before increasing their advantage. Spencer Prior and Mario Walsh combined well on the right flank and Walsh's pinpoint cross allowed David Crown to score with aplomb. It was a particularly gratifying strike for Crown as he had been heckled by the home crowd for being a former Reading player. Minutes later it was 4-0 when another assist from Mario Walsh allowed Crown to score his seventh goal of the new campaign.

Southend's breathtaking display left the home defence in total disarray and it was no real surprise when they conceded a second own goal a minute from time. Jason Cook's accurate corner saw centre-back Colin Smith finally outjump the lively Walsh. Unfortunately his firm header left his goalkeeper totally stranded as the ball crashed into the net for a fifth time.

A stunning performance by the Shrimpers saw the club secure their biggest away win since 1957 and the club were awarded the Barclays Performance of the Week with a local boys' club being presented with a cheque for £650.

ALDERSHOT 0   **SOUTHEND UNITED 5**
                                   Bennett, Brown (o.g.), Crown (2),
                                   Smith (o.g.)

 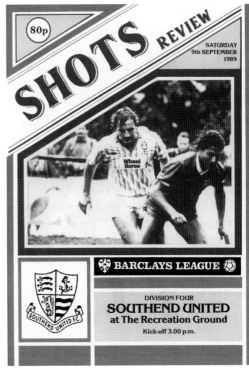

Above left: An inspirational performance by transfer-listed winger Gary Bennett paved the way for a big win at the Recreation Ground.

Aldershot: David Coles, Kevan Brown, Ian Phillips, Peter Coyne, Colin Smith, Steve Wignall, Jerry Williams, David Puckett, Dale Banton, Charlie Henry, Ian Stewart. Subs: Steve Claridge (for Brown) and Glen Burvill (for Wignall)

Southend United: Paul Sansome, Andy Dixon, Paul Roberts, Dave Martin, Spencer Prior, Martin Ling, Jason Cook, Peter Butler, David Crown, Mario Walsh, Gary Bennett. Subs: Paul Brush and Roy McDonough (not used)

SOUTHEND UNITED v. TOTTENHAM HOTSPUR

4 October 1989   Littlewoods Cup Second Round, Second Leg

Southend had climbed to the top of the Fourth Division following a 2-0 defeat of previous table-toppers Lincoln City. The Shrimpers were boasting a 100 per cent home record with five straight wins from the start of the season. However, Tottenham held a 1-0 first-leg lead after a Terry Fenwick goal had separated the two sides in a dour game at White Hart Lane on 20 September. It was hoped that Southend's magnificent home form would give the mighty Spurs a severe test at a packed Roots Hall. The majority of the 10,418 crowd would go home happy as the Shrimpers served up a memorable performance which vanquished a star-studded Tottenham line-up including Paul Gascoigne and new signing Gary Lineker, freshly arrived from Barcelona for £1.4 million.

Southend signalled their intentions to take the game to their more illustrious opponents as early as the second minute when Gary Bennett latched onto a great through ball by Roy McDonough, only to appear to be hauled down on the edge of the penalty area by Pat van den Hauwe. Referee Paul Danson waved play on and David Crown shot narrowly past Thorstvedt's left-hand post.

The Blues continued to press and a sustained attack on the South Bank goal saw Fenwick forced to concede a corner after five minutes. Jason Cook, a former Spurs apprentice, swung in the corner kick and Dave Martin out-jumped Fenwick to power home a downward header. Amazingly Southend had wiped out the first leg deficit in just five minutes.

Shell-shocked Spurs had their first meaningful attack on eight minutes when Paul Allen lofted a ball into the danger area and Spencer Prior completely missed his kick, allowing England international Gary Lineker to have a one-on-one with Paul Sansome. The former Millwall 'keeper stood up well and parried Lineker's shot. Gascoigne badly miscued the rebound, which went harmlessly wide.

On eleven minutes Crown burst clear from the Spurs defence and crossed to an unmarked McDonough. The veteran forward struck a sweet left-foot shot but the ball cannoned back off the crossbar with Erik Thorstvedt totally stranded. Four minutes later Blues had another great chance to take the lead when a great flick from Crown released midfielder Peter Butler, but as the Yorkshireman was about to shoot home Fenwick made a superb challenge to concede nothing more than a corner kick.

Spurs gradually found their passing game and on twenty-four minutes a long clearance from Erik Thorstvedt was not dealt with by Prior and Lineker was dismayed to see his shot clear Sansome's left-hand post. A minute later Nayim's twenty-five-yard effort was well handled by Sansome. From the resulting clearance Crown was again clean through, only to be hauled down by Gary Mabbutt, who was lucky to escape with only a verbal admonishment from the referee.

SOUTHEND UNITED 3   **TOTTENHAM HOTSPUR 2**

Martin, Bennett (2)   Allen, Nayim

SOUTHEND UNITED v. TOTTENHAM HOTSPUR

Dave Martin opens the scoring after five minutes. Roy McDonough and David Crown join in the celebrations.

On forty-one minutes the Blues increased their lead when Mabbutt failed to deal with a header into the box from Butler and Crown retrieved the loose ball. He put a left-footed pass back across the danger area allowing an onrushing Gary Bennett to prod home from close range.

Half-time approached with Southend amazingly 2-0 up against mighty Tottenham but, as so often happens, a lack of concentration a minute before the break saw the tie squared on aggregate. Paul Allen raced onto a neat flick from Lineker after a long ball from Fenwick had found the England man in space. Allen controlled the ball well and dispatched a low shot underneath Sansome's diving body. However, Spurs had another fright right on the half-time whistle when Mitchell Thomas fluffed his clearance, allowing Bennett to find Crown. His pass saw McDonough roll the ball into an empty net only to realise Crown had been flagged for a marginal offside decision.

Two minutes into the second half Bennett, who was playing with a badly broken nose after a first-half collision with Mabbutt, fired narrowly wide when well placed. On forty-nine minutes the match blew up into controversy, which would rumble on long after the final whistle. Southend captain Paul Roberts and Paul Stewart of Spurs jumped for the same ball. Stewart struck Roberts in the face with a vicious elbow and with referee Danson well placed only a couple of yards away he was left with little option but to dismiss Stewart for violent conduct. The Southend full-back was subsequently accused of cheating and won a High Court libel case against the *Sun* newspaper and was awarded undisclosed damages for defamation of character.

Despite their numerical disadvantage Spurs levelled the match at 2-2 after fifty-five minutes when Fenwick floated over a cross and substitute David Howells out-jumped Spencer Prior to head the

£1

Matchday Magazine 1989-1990

Matchday Magazine

SOUTHEND UNITED FOOTBALL CLUB

Matchday Magazine 1989-1990

Matchday Magazine 1989-1990

Matchday Magazine 1989-1990

Martin Ling runs at the Spurs defence at White Hart Lane

THE LITTLEWOODS CUP Round 2 2nd Leg
Wednesday, 4th October · Kick-Off 7.45pm

v TOTTENHAM HOTSPUR

MAIN SPONSOR 1989 - 1990
FIRHOLM BUILDERS
01-993 5838 Southend (0702) 433127

ball down to the Moroccan-born Spanish international Nayim. His exquisite body swerve totally bemused Andy Dixon and he had the easy task of beating Sansome from close range.

The match continued at a frantic pace: Martin was booked for a lunge on Howells and Lineker should have scored but headed narrowly wide from a Gascoigne cross. Southend took the lead again in the sixty-seventh minute. Paul Brush took a free-kick in the centre circle and McDonough flicked the ball on despite the close attentions of Mabbutt. The ball fell to unmarked Gary Bennett who gleefully shot home and went to celebrate with the home fans packed into the North Bank enclosure. Soon after, McDonough, no stranger to the referee's notebook, was yellow carded for a late challenge on Fenwick.

On seventy minutes Bennett was denied a hat-trick with a fine save from Thorstvedt. A minute later Crown hit the post with the Norwegian 'keeper beaten after Butler had dispossessed Howells with a typically tigerish tackle.

As the match headed towards extra time Spurs had opportunities to seal the match, Gascoigne dazzled the Southend defence but shot wide and later good work by Paul Walsh saw Lineker miss another good chance. The England striker then hit the post with an overhead kick following Mabbutt's flick-on from a Gascoigne set piece.

With the match tied at 3-3 on aggregate the rules stated that a period of extra time would ensue to determine a winner. If no further goals occurred the away goals rule would be enforced. This meant a goal-less extra time period would see the tie go to the Londoners. Southend had to score.

The first half of extra time was cagey with Spurs content to defend. However, Nayim nearly put the tie beyond doubt with his second goal, but he didn't see the linesman waving for an earlier offside. Southend were reduced to ten men when a late challenge on Howells by Roy McDonough down by the East Stand touchline saw the striker dismissed for the sixth time in his Southend career. Crown could have sealed a famous win in the second period of extra time but his late effort was denied by an outstanding save from Thorstvedt. Spurs also had a late chance but substitute Paul Walsh could only find the side netting when well placed.

So Southend achieved a famous and richly deserved victory over a First Division side but sadly the away goals rule meant it was Spurs that would progress to the next round of the Littlewoods Cup.

Southend United: Paul Sansome, Andy Dixon, Paul Roberts, David Martin, Spencer Prior, Paul Brush, Jason Cook, Peter Butler, David Crown, Roy McDonough, Gary Bennett. Sub: Mario Walsh (for Cook) and Justin Edinburgh (for Dixon)

Tottenham Hotspur: Erik Thorstvedt, Mitchell Thomas, Pat van den Hauwe, Terry Fenwick, Paul Allen, Gary Mabbutt, Nayim, Paul Gascoigne, Paul Stewart, Gary Lineker, Steve Sedgley. Subs: Paul Walsh (for Allen) and David Howells (for Thomas)

PETERBOROUGH UNITED v. SOUTHEND UNITED

5 May 1990   Football League Fourth Division

Southend went into the final game of this season knowing three points at London Road would mean promotion from the Four Division at the first time of asking, having suffered relegation at the end of the previous campaign.

It was a tension-filled encounter that was not helped by the referee, Mike Reed of Birmingham, who gave an erratic performance and compounded the agony for Southend supporters on a sweltering day by contriving to add on no less than seven minutes of injury time at the end of the game.

Southend took the game to the home side and opened the scoring early on when star striker David Crown unusually found the net with his weaker left foot. The home side fought back and Paul Sansome was called into action to deny an equalising goal for both David Riley and Worrell Sterling. On twenty-two minutes young full-back Dean Austin hacked a goal-bound header from Noel Luke off the line to preserve the Shrimpers' slender advantage. However, Blues eased the situation by scoring again midway through the opening half. It was left to top scorer Crown to settle the side down. His twenty-third goal of the season resulted from a neat pass from Martin Ling. Crown controlled the ball well and his right-footed drive just eluded the despairing dive of Posh's young goalkeeper Paul Crichton. Despite a nervous end to the opening half when Steve Osborne shot narrowly past the post, Southend went into the interval with their precious lead intact.

Peterborough reduced the arrears just four minutes into the restart when veteran skipper Mick Halsall bundled home a loose ball that really should have been cleared. It was then a backs-to-the-wall effort as the Southend defence was forced to withstand tremendous pressure from the home side. As an attacking force Southend rarely looked like increasing their lead. Southend's youngsters tackled as if their lives depended on it, Austin and Edwards standing firm alongside veteran centre-back Paul Clark, who was outstanding in this game and throughout his richly deserved testimonial season. In midfield, Paul Smith, making only the eighth start of his fledgling career, was immense and gave a performance that belied his tender years.

After an interminable wait for the final whistle, 1,500 mentally exhausted travelling Blues supporters celebrated raucously as promotion was confirmed. Southend finished third behind Exeter City and Grimsby while Stockport County missed out by a single point. The now-defunct Maidstone United finished fifth, a further point behind the Shrimpers.

PETERBOROUGH UNITED 1	SOUTHEND UNITED 2
Halsall	Crown (2)

PETERBOROUGH UNITED v. SOUTHEND UNITED

A rare left-foot shot from David Crown opened the scoring.

Peterborough United: Paul Crichton, Noel Luke, Phil Crosby, Mick Halsall, David Robinson, Keith Oakes, Worrell Sterling, Mark Hine, Steve Osborne, David Riley, Garry Butterworth. Subs: Martin Moore (for Crosby) and Dale Watkins (for Hine)

Southend United: Paul Sansome, Dean Austin, Justin Edinburgh, Dave Martin, Andy Edwards, Paul Clark, Martin Ling, Paul Smith, David Crown, Ian Benjamin, Peter Butler. Subs: Peter Daley (for Smith) and Steve Tilson (not used)

SOUTHEND UNITED v. ALDERSHOT

6 November 1990   Leyland DAF Cup Group Match

Southend United equalled their record victory in a one-sided Leyland DAF Cup-tie at Roots Hall. Southend were in the Third Division and were beginning the push for an ultimately successful promotion challenge for the second campaign running. Aldershot were a lowly Fourth Division side who would subsequently fold in March 1992.

The Shrimpers started brightly with John Cornwell signalling intentions, shooting over from thirty yards in only the third minute. A minute later and John Sheffield's goal was breached for the first time. Peter Cawley, playing in place of an injured Paul Clark, swept a searching ball out to Steve Tilson on the left flank. The skilful midfielder turned his marker and his cross-cum-shot found the corner of the net with Sheffield put off by a lunging Ian Benjamin who failed to touch the ball but caused enough distraction to open the scoring. The Blues went two-up after thirteen minutes when Chris Powell cleared the ball to Andy Ansah. His cross found Tilson who managed to stoop low and backhead the ball past Sheffield.

Southend dominated the play but during an untidy spell, punctured by several infringements and stoppages, Benjamin was cautioned following a late tackle on Steve Wignall. The veteran defender was unable to continue and was replaced by pacy winger Dale Banton.

The Shots fell further behind after twenty-five minutes when a superb Tilson corner was flicked on at the near post by John Cornwell. The header fell to Brett Angell, who chested the ball down and half-volleyed it on target, and although Sheffield got one hand to the ball he was unable to keep it out.

From the restart Aldershot had their first chance when David Puckett blazed over having been sent clear by Charlie Henry. Angell had a good chance to make it 4-0 on the half-hour mark when Ansah put in a deep cross only for Angell to slice his volley well wide. The tall striker did not have to wait very long for his next opportunity, as barely a minute later a long clearance from goalkeeper Paul Sansome was met by Ansah. His infield pass to Cornwell saw the blond midfielder float a lofted pass over the Shots' backline and Angell and Benjamin raced after the ball. Sheffield was first to the loose ball but completely missed his kick, allowing Angell to sidefoot into an unguarded net.

On thirty-seven minutes Kevan Brown connected well to send in a shot from thirty yards, although his shot was dealt with comfortably by Sansome. The former Millwall custodian cleared his lines and, after a shocking piece of defending by Leigh Cooper, Tilson saw his shot spilled by Sheffield, although Brown managed to hack the ball clear before Angell descended.

Southend went five up after forty-one minutes when a deft Tilson through ball released Ansah, unusually, down the left flank. The tricky winger was quickly closed down but a swift interchange of passes with Benjamin saw Ansah hit a sweet left-foot cross which allowed Angell to outjump Cooper to head home for a first-half hat-trick.

SOUTHEND UNITED 10	**ALDERSHOT 1**
Tilson (3), Angell (4), Prior, Ansah, Benjamin	Banton

Steve Tilson (bottom right) loops a brilliant header in against Aldershot for the second goal.

The second half started in much the same vein with John Cornwell blasting over after forty-seven minutes. Combative midfielder Peter Butler was cautioned a minute later following a hefty tackle on Ian Stewart.

Southend's sixth goal came on fifty-six minutes when Tilson delivered another first-class corner kick deep into the danger area. John Flower headed clear but Tilson returned the ball with a vengance, allowing an unmarked Spencer Prior to head home. A minute later Henry was booked for dissent when he refused after several warnings to take a free-kick from the correct place. After sixty-nine minutes Southend went seven goals up when yet another Tilson corner saw Ian Benjamin's goal-bound header hacked off the line by Stewart, only for Ansah to almost disdainfully half-volley the ball into the net. Six minutes later Angell claimed his fourth goal of the evening when he latched on to a Sansome clearance. He passed to Butler whose perfectly weighted return ball allowed Angell to clip the ball over the hapless Sheffield.

Ian Benjamin finally got on the scoresheet after eighty minutes. Chris Powell swung in a cross and Ansah was able to turn his marker. Sheffield managed to block his shot but the ball looped up onto the crossbar. To the young 'keeper's dismay the ball fell kindly to Benjamin who stooped to head home from little more than a yard.

By now everyone was trying to get onto the scoresheet and Butler rained in a powerful shot from twenty-five yards. Sheffield could only parry the ball, which was retrieved by Benjamin. The veteran striker squared to Tilson who was able to turn Whitlock easily and shoot home to send the Blues into double figures.

After one-way traffic for eighty-four minutes, Aldershot promptly scored the best goal of the night. Whitlock hit a free-kick from deep in his own half, and Puckett was released down the flank. He passed to Banton who hit a sweet shot past Sansome, who perhaps could be forgiven as he had

been a virtual spectator for the entire game. The closing minutes saw Cornwell's header cleared off the line by Adrian Randall. Randall then forced Sansome into a smart save in the final minute.

Aldershot's shell-shocked manager, Len Walker, commented afterwards that it was 'the most embarrassing match of my career, I have never lost to double figures, not even when I was in the Cubs!' It was a real pity that this stellar performance of total domination came in this unfashionable competition and only a hardy 1,281 of the Blues' faithful could say 'I was there!'

Southend United: Paul Sansome, Dean Austin, Chris Powell, John Cornwell, Spencer Prior, Steve Tilson, Peter Cawley, Peter Butler, Andy Ansah, Ian Benjamin, Brett Angell. Subs: Andy Edwards and Adam Locke (not used)

Aldershot: John Sheffield, Kevan Brown, Leigh Cooper, Adrian Randall, Steve Wignall, John Flower, Mark Whitlock, David Puckett, Jerry Williams, Charlie Henry, Ian Stewart. Subs: Dale Banton (for Wignall) and Glen Burvill (not used)

Southend United v. Torquay United

The scoreline in this match was truly remarkable bearing in mind that with only thirty-five minutes left the game was goal-less! A turgid first half saw Southend's long-ball tactics being swallowed up easily by the sizeable visiting defence. The half-time break could not come soon enough and manager Dave Webb reorganised the side, instructing his charges to play the ball to feet and attack down the channels.

Torquay's aerially dominant defence was turned into a ponderous, disorganised unit as the side managed by former Blues championship-winning boss Dave Smith self-destructed in spectacular fashion. The floodgates opened after fifty-five minutes when centre-back Andy Edwards hit an unstoppable dipping volley past Gareth Howells in the visiting goal. Eight minutes later a harsh penalty was awarded when Peter Whiston was adjudged to have upended Adam Locke on one of his typically pacy runs. Dave Martin made no mistake from the penalty spot. The result was put beyond doubt when Andy Ansah scored twice in two minutes in the sixty-ninth and seventieth minutes. First, a pass of extreme quality from Steve Tilson split the two centre-backs and Ansah's pace allowed him to beat Howells to the ball and slide the ball into an unguarded net. Then Tilson and Powell combined to release Ansah again and the tiny forward produced a replica finish to make the score 4-0. On seventy-two minutes Southend made it 5-0 when Dave Martin rose highest to nod in a well-placed corner from the skilful Steve Tilson.

Southend were now in showboating mode with some audacious skills heaping the embarrassment on the visitors and particularly their manager, an all-time favourite with the Roots Hall faithful. The Southend team were clearly in no mood to take things easy and must have been looking to beat the record-equalling 10-1 scoreline achieved three months earlier in the same competition against luckless Aldershot.

The sixth goal came on seventy-eight minutes and was started deep in his own half by Paul Clark. His outrageous ball to the right flank released Adam Locke in acres of space. The winger raced forward, beat two defenders and squared the ball into the path of substitute Brett Angell who finished with consummate ease. The rout was completed on eighty-six minutes when a mesmeric move between Powell, Tilson and Angell allowed Andy Ansah to complete his first hat-trick in senior football.

A clearly shell-shocked Torquay side trudged off the pitch and went straight into a lengthy inquest in a locked visitor's dressing room. A beleaguered Dave Smith eventually emerged to face the music and when asked what had happened to his side in the second half he offered a good example of his laconic wit by saying 'they scored more goals than us'. Later he would reflect on the match as the most humiliating of his lengthy career.

SOUTHEND UNITED 7   **TORQUAY UNITED 0**
  Edwards, Martin (2, 1 pen),
  Ansah (3), Angell

SOUTHEND UNITED v. TORQUAY UNITED

Above left: A first senior hat-trick for Andy Ansah.

Southend United: Paul Sansome, Dean Austin, Chris Powell, Dave Martin, Andy Edwards, Steve Tilson, Paul Clark, Peter Butler, Andy Ansah, Ian Benjamin, Adam Locke. Subs: Brett Angell (for Benjamin) and John Cornwell (not used)

Torquay United: Gareth Howells, Paul Holmes, John Uzzell, Peter Whiston, Matt Elliott, Russell Musker, Paul Smith, Micky Holmes, Tommy Tynan, Dean Edwards, Mark Loram. Subs: Chris Myers (for Musker) and Wes Saunders (for Micky Holmes)

BURY v. SOUTHEND UNITED

4 May 1991   Football League Third Division

A large contingent of Southend fans congregated at the Cemetery End of Gigg Lane in the knowledge that three points from that afternoon's game would guarantee Second Division football for the first time in the club's long and decidedly inglorious eighty-five-year history. It was to turn out to be a highly fraught but ultimately triumphant afternoon.

Bury nearly gifted Southend an early lead when after two minutes Peter Valentine sliced a long throw from Christian Hyslop towards his own goal. However, a swift piece of goalkeeping from Gary Kelly spared the veteran centre-back's blushes. Southend kept up the pressure on the Shakers' defence with a succession of early corners.

Wide-midfielder Adam Locke was booked just six minutes into the game when he mistimed a challenge on Colin Greenhall. The situation was worsened by the reaction of some of the other Bury players, which undoubtedly contributed to the waving of a yellow card. The Blues should have taken the lead after twelve minutes but Andy Ansah miscued badly, shooting high and wide after a poor clearance by Liam Robinson.

The first half progressed with some scrappy play punctuated by numerous free-kicks for niggling fouls and Bury's well-drilled offside trap. Southend dominated possession with the home side seemingly happy to try and score from a counterattack.

The next chance came on forty minutes when from Paul Clark's long free-kick, Dave Martin headed the ball back down to Hyslop. The blond left-back crossed to Ansah who flicked the ball on to Brett Angell but an unkind bounce on Bury's well-worn penalty area saw the big striker miss his chance and Kelly was able to gather.

Two minutes later saw the odds stacked firmly against the Shrimpers. Ansah was tugged back by Greenhall but Butler's resulting free-kick was cleared to David Lee. The little winger evaded Martin's tackle but was clattered to the ground by a high and late challenge from Southend's Irish centre-back Pat Scully. The incident took place right in front of the Bury bench and the whole of Bury's staff and substitutes erupted with fury. In truth the tackle was bad and referee Paul Vanes had little option but to show Scully a red card. At that moment all Blues fans were praying that the team could hold on for a goal-less draw and get the remaining points required in the final two games of the season at home to Leyton Orient and Brentford.

The first chance of the second half came on the hour and fell to Southend but following Kelly's spill of an Adam Locke cross, Angell was unable to reach the loose ball. After seventy-one minutes Valentine was booked for a brutal swipe at Ansah but just two minutes later Bury had a great chance to take the lead. However, young forward Kevin Hulme blazed over when well placed.

BURY 0   **SOUTHEND UNITED 1**
                                                  Benjamin

Irishman Pat Scully was red-carded for a rash challenge.

BURY F.C.

Macpherson PAINTS

MAIN CLUB
SPONSORS

M   M

SATURDAY, 4th MAY, 1991
SOUTHEND UNITED
BARCLAYS LEAGUE - DIVISION THREE
KICK-OFF 3.00 p.m.

Today's Match Sponsor: MILLIKEN CONTRACT CARPETS

£1.00

BURY v. SOUTHEND UNITED

Bury tried to make the numerical advantage tell and pressed forward in search of a goal. On seventy-five minutes a hopeful shot from Robinson dipped alarmingly and Sansome did well to tip the ball onto the crossbar and over for a corner. From the resulting corner Valentine headed narrowly over the bar.

Four minutes later Sansome saved well from Robinson who had been sent clear with a great defence-splitting pass from Charlie Bishop. Then, on eighty-three minutes, decidedly against the run of play, it happened! Kelly's goal kick was headed back by Martin, Ansah ran at the Bury defence and got a lucky break when the ball bounced back to him off Greenhall's shin. He switched onto his weaker left foot and his scuffed cross managed to find veteran striker Ian Benjamin with his back to goal. He managed to swivel past Roger Stanislaus and while falling backwards scooped a low left-foot drive into the corner of the Bury net. A classic and timeless moment that sent the Blues faithful into raptures behind the goal. A minute later Hulme was booked for a terrible lunge on Martin and Southend tried to wind the clock down by introducing Chris Powell and John Cornwell as late substitutes.

After an interminable wait the referee blew his whistle and the celebrations began. A now-suited Scully was first onto the pitch to thank his teammates for surviving against all odds following his earlier indiscretion. The Southend players ran to the Cemetery End to thank the noisy supporters who were now hanging off the security fencing and generally going bananas.

A memorable afternoon and justified reward for a special Southend United team.

Bury: Gary Kelly, Charlie Bishop, Roger Stanislaus, Ronnie Mauge, Peter Valentine, Colin Greenhall, David Lee, Liam Robinson, Kevin Hulme, Phil Parkinson, Mark Kearney. Subs: Mike Sheron (for Mauge) and Andy Feeney (not used)

Southend United: Paul Sansome, Dean Austin, Christian Hyslop, Dave Martin, Pat Scully, Adam Locke, Paul Clark, Peter Butler, Andy Ansah, Ian Benjamin, Brett Angell. Subs: Chris Powell (for Locke) and John Cornwell (for Angell)

SOUTHEND UNITED v. CHARLTON ATHLETIC

26 October 1991   Football League Second Division

This was another extraordinary game, which was directly due to some eccentric refereeing. Kelvin Morton awarded three penalties, sent off two players and the Charlton manager and even found the time to show four yellow cards in a tempestuous match.

The game had been delayed by fifteen minutes as Charlton fans were stuck in a traffic jam on the M25, but the late-arriving fans must have wondered if it was worth the effort as their table-topping side looked a pale shadow of its usual self in the opening half.

Southend dominated possession in the opening period but rarely tested Bob Bolder in the visitors' goal. The first noteworthy incident occurred on thirty-four minutes when livewire winger Andy Ansah burst into the penalty area only to be upended by a heavy challenge from Steve Gatting. Gatting was cautioned for the tackle and Charlton boss Alan Curbishley was ordered from the dugout after remonstrating with the linesmen over the decision. He was later charged with using foul and abusive language.

Southend had missed their previous seven spot kicks and several players had tried but failed to end the jinx. This time right-back Dean Austin was handed the responsibility. Despite an awkward delay due to Charlton's vehement protests, Austin coolly slotted the ball into the corner of the net.

Tempers were fraying rapidly on both sides due to a string of bizarre decisions and it came as no surprise a minute from half-time when Gatting was dismissed for a second cautionable offence when he upended Ian Benjamin just outside the penalty area.

Charlton's joint-managers, Curbishley and Steve Gritt, must have earned their keep during the interval as the Valiants were unrecognisable after the restart from the lethargic eleven that laboured through the opening period.

Charlton tore into the Southend rearguard and goalkeeper Paul Sansome had to make a string of saves to keep his side afloat. He was helpless, however, on fifty-three minutes when lanky striker Carl Leaburn outjumped everybody to head home a well-flighted corner kick.

The next strange decision came on sixty-two minutes when Spencer Prior was red-carded, without a previous caution, for a tussle with Garry Nelson that saw both players fall to the ground in a heap. To make matters worse for the Blues, Morton adjudged that the incident had occurred inside the penalty area and the afternoon's second penalty was awarded. Full-back Darren Pitcher stepped up to take the kick but Sansome made a full-length dive to parry the shot to safety.

Remarkably, Morton pointed the spot again just three minutes later when Dean Austin apparently fouled Robert Lee. Pitcher was reluctant to try again so Colin Walsh stepped to face Sansome. He

SOUTHEND UNITED 1	CHARLTON ATHLETIC 1
Austin (pen)	Leaburn

SOUTHEND UNITED v. CHARLTON ATHLETIC

 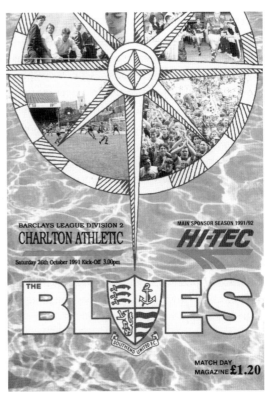

Above left: Full-back Dean Austin ended the club's penalty jinx.

sent the Blues' 'keeper the wrong way but was aghast to see his kick hit the post and rebound into play before being cleared by Pat Scully.

Blues held on for a valuable point despite some heavy pressure and Sansome turned in a stunning performance to deny Leaburn and Nelson on numerous occasions.

Southend United: Paul Sansome, Dean Austin, Chris Powell, Keith Jones, Pat Scully, Spencer Prior, Andy Ansah, John Cornwell, Steve Tilson, Ian Benjamin, Brett Angell. Subs: Adam Locke (for Angell) and Mark Hall (not used)

Charlton Athletic: Bob Bolder, Darren Pitcher, Scott Minto, Andy Peake, Simon Webster, Steve Gatting, Rob Lee, John Bumstead, Carl Leaburn, Garry Nelson, Colin Walsh. Subs: Anthony Barness and Alex Dyer (not used)

Southend United v. Newcastle United

It seems an unlikely scoreline nowadays but Southend were a powerful team in 1992 and because of this early kick-off they briefly topped the old Second Division, giving them the highest placing in their long history. Wins for Blackburn and Ipswich later in the afternoon meant Blues would finish the day in third place.

This was a devastating result for the Geordies and days later their Argentinean World Cup winner, Osvaldo Ardiles, was sacked as Newcastle manager.

Southend got off to a great start, opening the scoring after two minutes when leading scorer Brett Angell robbed Alan Thompson before shooting goalwards. His shot took a wicked deflection off Kevin Scott and left Tommy Wright completely wrong-footed. The Blues should have increased their lead on fourteen minutes but Ian Benjamin's volley produced a first-class save from Tommy Wright. Minutes later Sansome did the same at the other end, turning a powerful shot from Steve Watson around the post. Benjamin squandered another chance before Steve Howey hit the post from a Gavin Peacock centre. Blues took the game by the scruff of the neck just before half-time when Keith Jones drilled home his first goal for the club from the edge of the box.

After the restart Andy Ansah's pace created himself a golden chance for a third goal but he shot weakly at Wright when well placed. He made up for his error in the fifty-fifth minute when he rose well to meet a Keith Jones cross, his header just eluding the outstretched arm of the visiting goalkeeper. Newcastle then slipped into gear and Lee Clark saw his shot hit the post and in a crazy spell of sixty seconds Chris Powell twice saved his goalkeeper's blushes by heading goal-bound efforts off the line.

The fourth goal of a scintillating performance went to Brett Angell, who latched on to Matt Appleby's weak back pass before coolly rounding Tommy Wright and steering the ball home.

The game was witnessed by a bumper Roots Hall crowd of 9,458, the majority of whom will always remember the day the mighty Shrimpers silenced the Toon Army.

SOUTHEND UNITED 4   **NEWCASTLE UNITED 0**
Angell (2), Jones, Ansah

SOUTHEND UNITED v. NEWCASTLE UNITED

Above left: Brett Angell scored two goals against mighty Newcastle.

Southend United: Paul Sansome, Dean Austin, Chris Powell, Keith Jones, Pat Scully, Spencer Prior, Andy Ansah, John Cornwell, Steve Tilson, Ian Benjamin, Brett Angell. Subs: Peter Butler (for Jones) and Adam Locke (not used)

Newcastle United: Tommy Wright, Steve Watson, Paul Bodin, Alan Thompson, Kevin Scott, Matt Appleby, Lee Clark, Gavin Peacock, David Kelly, Steve Howey, Lee Makel. Subs: Andy Hunt (for Kelly) and Darren Bradshaw (not used)

Southend United v. Notts County

21 November 1992   Football League Division One

Southend fans could have been mistaken for assuming a hasty signing of an unknown player was the act of a desperate man. Colin Murphy, the deeply unpopular Southend manager, plucked twenty-one-year-old Stan Collymore from the Crystal Palace reserve team. So hasty was the loan signing that cries of 'who?' rang out when the tannoy announcer announced 'number ten: Stan Collymore' just prior to the kick-off of this match with Notts County.

Murphy was a man under intense pressure, with some 400 Blues fans boycotting the game and standing outside calling for his resignation. His bizarre, rambling programme notes and unusual training methods had bemused the team and they were struggling at the wrong end of the Division One table. The boycott and general apathy saw a paltry crowd of 3,219, the lowest at Roots Hall for two years. The Blues' faithful were also mourning the loss of cult hero Ian Benjamin, who had been sold to Luton Town a week before. However, the signing of Stan Collymore was to prove to be a pivotal moment in the history of Southend United Football Club.

A day of very heavy rain saw Murphy also draft in eighteen-year-old youngsters Steve Brown and Scott Ashenden into his beleaguered side. Southend attacked from the off and Collymore's pace and ability were evident from the start. Southend took the lead after only four minutes when Andy Edwards' inch-perfect cross was headed home by Steve Brown for his first senior goal. The Shrimpers poured forward and doubled their lead after seventeen minutes when Pat Scully's penetrating free-kick was only half cleared by the Magpies' defence. Collymore met the clearance full on the volley and unleashed an unstoppable shot past the stranded Steve Cherry in the visitors' goal.

Blues continued to dominate and the rare County attacks were snuffed out by the defence of Scully and Spencer Prior. However, a lifeline was given to the visitors in the thirty-second minute when Andy Sussex was adjudged to have bought down Kevin Bartlett in the penalty area. Robbie Turner took the spot kick but blazed high over the crossbar. It was to prove a costly mistake as a minute after the restart Southend put the game out of sight when Collymore drove in from the edge of the penalty area.

Southend should have extended their advantage after sixty-three minutes but young Scott Ashenden showed his inexperience and shot wide in front of a gaping goal. County reduced the arrears three minutes later when a scramble in the home penalty box resulted in Bartlett stabbing the ball past Sansome from close range. Collymore was inches away from claiming a debut hat-trick in the seventieth minute but his fierce shot cannoned back off the crossbar.

The game petered out as the conditions grew increasingly treacherous but Collymore looked like he was going to score every time he gained possession. The 'stay-away' fans had missed a real treat as Blues secured their first win in eleven matches.

SOUTHEND UNITED 3
Brown, Collymore (2)

NOTTS COUNTY 1
Bartlett

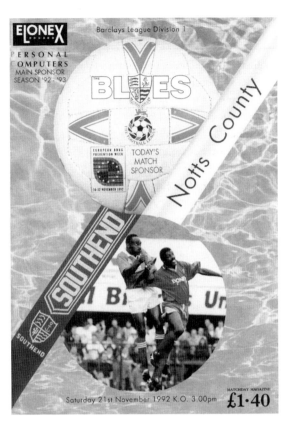

Above left: Stan Collymore's memorable debut against Notts County.

Collymore would score another sixteen goals in only thirty-two matches and mesmerised Blues supporters for a fleeting time. By the end of the season Murphy was gone, victim of a 'red card' protest from supporters as well as some of his own players who hid the 'red cards' under their training tops, much to the delight of the crowd. His replacement, Barry Fry, got even greater performances from Collymore as the team finally cleared the relegation trapdoor. Collymore departed in the close season but Fry's acumen in the transfer market ensured the Blues would secure £3.57 million for their prized asset. Stan Collymore would rise to stardom and become one of the most talked-about players of the modern era.

Southend United: Paul Sansome, Andy Edwards, Christian Hyslop, John Cornwell, Pat Scully, Spencer Prior, Adam Locke, Andy Sussex, Steve Brown, Stan Collymore, Scott Ashenden. Subs: Steve Tilson and Francisco Cagigao (not used)

Notts County: Steve Cherry, Chris Short, Dean Thomas, Charlie Palmer, Rob Turner, Don O'Riordan, Mark Draper, Andy Williams, Gary Lund, Kevin Bartlett, Paul Devlin. Subs: Steve Slawson (for Devlin) and Shaun Murphy (for O'Riordan)

Southend United v. West Ham United

7 April 1993   Football League Division One

A large crowd of 12,813 packed into Roots Hall for this local derby, which was Barry Fry's second game in charge of the Blues since taking over the hot seat from the hapless Colin Murphy. The club had been staring relegation in the face when they finally dispensed with Murphy's services and survival chances were rated as slim at best. However, the mercurial Fry galvanised the squad and achieved an unlikely survival on the last day of the campaign.

Fry had switched Spencer Prior to right-back and bought Pat Scully into the side to partner Andy Edwards at the heart of the defence. Paul Sansome's red card at Notts County meant that twenty-one-year-old understudy Simon Royce came in for his first start of the season. The youngster signed from Heybridge Swifts rose to the occasion superbly and gave a commanding performance as well as producing a string of wonderful saves.

The opening exchanges were tense and it was disappointing to note the taunting of Stan Collymore by visiting supporters. The skilful front man however had the last laugh when he was the integral part of the game's only goal.

The goal came in the thirty-second minute after Southend had weathered a spell of intense pressure from the Londoners. Keith Jones had picked up a loose ball near the halfway line. His superb thirty-five-yard pass found Collymore in space. He took control of the ball at pace and drove past Steve Potts. His cross was perfect for the onrushing Brett Angell, whose shot found the net off the underside of the crossbar.

Southend went in at half-time with only a narrow lead but looked by far the better-balanced side. Collymore's skill, pace and strength dominated the second half and he had two shots that went narrowly past Miklosko's posts. The visitors pressed forward in the final fifteen minutes but Royce did extremely well to keep his goal intact. He twice kept David Speedie from levelling the scores. First he held on to a low drive from the Scottish international and then bravely dived at his feet to rescue the ball off his toes when a goal looked certain. The last real chance, however, fell to the home side in the eighty-fifth minute when a sublime cross from Steve Tilson gave young midfielder Paul Smith the chance to score. With Miklosko stranded the ball hit the bar and was cleared to safety by Tim Breacker.

A fine victory against bitter rivals gave the Blues a second straight win under the mercurial Fry and was the footing for a successful pull away from the relegation zone. It was also a severe blow to West Ham's promotion hopes, although they eventually recovered to finish second behind champions Newcastle United.

SOUTHEND UNITED 1   **WEST HAM UNITED 0**

Angell

SOUTHEND UNITED v. WEST HAM UNITED

Above left: Young Simon Royce turned in an inspired performance to thwart local rivals West Ham.

Southend United: Simon Royce, Andy Edwards, Chris Powell, Keith Jones, Pat Scully, Spencer Prior, Andy Ansah, Paul Smith, Steve Tilson, Stan Collymore, Brett Angell. Subs: Andy Sussex and Mark Hall (not used)

West Ham United: Ludek Miklosko, Tim Breacker, Julian Dicks, Steve Potts, Tony Gale, Ian Bishop, Mark Robson, Peter Butler, David Speedie, Colin Foster, Kevin Keen. Subs: Matt Holmes and Kenny Brown (not used)

MILLWALL v. SOUTHEND UNITED

In life just occasionally it is great to rain on somebody else's parade. A superb Southend display well and truly ruined the celebration of the first competitive fixture at Millwall's shiny new home at The New Den. What made the game even better was the fact it was televised live on LWT.

Millwall had moved about half a mile from their menacing old ground in Cold Blow Lane. Their new ground was situated in an area known as Senegal Fields and the 20,000-capacity venue was erected in just fifty-seven weeks. The late John Smith, leader of the Labour Party, performed the ribbon-cutting ceremony on 4 August before an inauguration match against Sporting Lisbon.

Southend's prospects for the game were not great, having just been beaten 2-0 at home by Third Division Barnet in the Coca-Cola Cup and manager Barry Fry was missing four regulars, Keith Jones, Mick Bodley, Pat Scully and Gary Poole, all out with injuries. Fry handed a debut to new signing Jason Lee, bought for £150,000 from Lincoln, who had been suspended for the opening two matches of the campaign.

The game got off to a highly competitive start when in the fourth minute Millwall's Keith Stevens was forced to leave the field for some seven minutes while he had six stitches in a gaping head wound following a robust challenge from Jason Lee.

After six minutes Brett Angell was bundled over by Millwall's American goalkeeper Kasey Keller on the edge of the penalty area. Free-kick specialist Andy Sussex, however, could only fire the ball into the steadfast Millwall defensive wall. Four minutes later a silky run by winger Ricky Otto resulted in a deft through ball for Jason Lee, but the debutant could only fire straight at Keller in the Millwall goal. A minute later another blistering run by Otto was spoilt by a tame shot. From Keller's clearance Millwall had their first chance, with Ian Bogie blazing over from twenty-five yards.

On eighteen minutes Millwall really should have opened the scoring when Tony Dolby crossed to John Kerr. However, a great challenge from Andy Edwards scuppered the chance. Millwall duly opened the scoring on twenty-one minutes when Ian Dawes hit a high clearance downfield and Bressington's clearance was picked up by Bogie. He sent Kerr clear and Bressington was unable to prevent the pacy striker from slotting the ball past Sansome with a low left-footed drive. Ironically John Kerr had also scored the opening goal in the Sporting Lisbon game to register both the first goal and first competitive goal at the new venue.

Southend had a great chance to equalise after twenty-eight minutes when Andy Ansah passed to Lee. His flick found Angell well placed and the former Stockport striker forced Keller to parry his fierce shot. Kenny Cunningham affected the clearance and the chance was gone. A minute later great work by Derek Payne resulted in a pinpoint cross to Lee but his shot was superbly saved by Millwall's overworked custodian.

MILLWALL 1   **SOUTHEND UNITED 4**

Kerr   Lee, Otto, Mooney,

              Ansah

Millwall v. Southend United

Jason Lee spoiled Millwall's ground-opening match.

After thirty-three minutes Payne chipped the ball into the danger area but Ansah's snap shot hit Keller's left-hand post. Unbelievably, the ball came out to Angell who contrived to hit the same post when faced with an open goal. However, Southend's sustained pressure paid off when they equalised after thirty-five minutes. Full-back Adam Locke's corner to the near post was met by Jason Lee who managed to get goal-side of Tony McCarthy. His downward header gave Keller no chance. Two minutes later Millwall broke and from Andy Roberts' cross, American Bruce Murray headed against Sansome's crossbar.

Just before half-time Lee's running battle with Millwall's hardman Keith Stevens resulted in a yellow card for the Southend man after one foul too many for referee Keren Barratt.

The second half began with more Blues pressure, Brett Angell heading narrowly wide from a Derek Payne cross. After fifty-two minutes Gavin Maguire and the hot-headed but outrageously talented Ricky Otto were booked following a touchline scuffle. Southend took the lead on fifty-five

LIONS
v SOUTHEND UTD

SUNDAY 22 AUGUST 1993

KICK OFF 3PM

1993-94 FIRST SEASON

DIVISION ONE

OFFICIAL PROGRAMME £1.50

AT THE NEW DEN

minutes when Locke won possession deep in his own half. He played a tame-looking through ball which was totally misjudged by Stevens. This gave Lee the chance to play an accurate square ball to Otto who did well to net under great pressure from Cunningham. Three minutes later Sussex drove a thirty-five-yard free-kick, awarded for a shove on Lee, narrowly past the Lions' post. Former Millwall 'keeper Paul Sansome pulled off a marvellous block from a close-range effort from Ian Bogie after sixty-three minutes. A couple of minutes later Millwall's Andy Roberts found his way into the referee's notebook following a nasty, studs-out challenge on Andy Ansah.

The match swung decisively on seventy-one minutes when Sansome produced another wonder save to thwart Kerr and from his huge clearance, McCarthy and Stevens left the ball to each other allowing substitute Tommy Mooney to gently guide the ball past a stranded Kasey Keller.

Southend then absorbed a tremendous spell of Millwall pressure and sealed a famous win on eighty-one minutes. Payne released Otto on the left flank and his accurate cross found Ansah who had crept unmarked in between Dawes and Stevens. His powerful downward header found the corner of the net past Keller's despairing dive.

Millwall's famous fighting spirit was broken and their players left the pitch to a crescendo of booing. At the far end Southend's brave warriors thanked the large contingent of travelling fans for their noisy support. Jason Lee was nominated Man of the Match by LWT's commentator and future Southend coach Theo Foley. Southend's irrepressible manager Barry Fry was thrilled with his charges' performance and quipped 'we murdered them from start to finish!' Too true Barry, too true.

Millwall: Kasey Keller, Kenny Cunningham, Ian Dawes, Gavin Maguire, Tony McCarthy, Keith Stevens, Andy Roberts, Iain Bogie, Bruce Murray, John Kerr, Tony Dolby. Subs: Richard Huxford (for Dolby), John Byrne (for Murray) and Carl Emberson (not used)

Southend United: Paul Sansome, Adam Locke, Chris Powell, Andy Edwards, Andy Sussex, Graham Bressington, Andy Ansah, Derek Payne, Jason Lee, Ricky Otto, Brett Angell. Subs: Tommy Mooney (for Angell), Jonathan Hunt (for Locke) and Simon Royce (not used)

A.C. FIORENTINA v. SOUTHEND UNITED

12 October 1993   Anglo-Italian Cup Group Game

When Southend qualified for the Anglo-Italian Cup they could not have expected a tougher baptism than an away tie to fallen giants Fiorentina. *La Viola* had been relegated to Serie B for the first time in fifty-four years but had managed to keep the vast majority of their expensively assembled, £64 million squad together, including Argentinian superstar Gabriel Batistuta.

Two hundred Southend supporters made their way to Florence and greeted their bemused hosts at the Artemio Franchi stadium with a playful 'you're not famous anymore' chant. However, parity was only temporary as the hosts slickly took the lead after eight minutes. Mauro Zironelli played a sublime through ball to Batistuta and the skilful forward ghosted past Bressington and Powell and scored with ease into the far corner of the net. Giacomo Banchelli then had a chance to double the *Viola*'s lead but Sansome did well to block his shot with his legs. Southend then thought they had scored an unexpected equaliser when Angell forced the ball past Scalabrelli only to see the linesman's flag calling played back for a late offside decision. Powell had a shot well saved and Keith Jones was on the verge of heading home from Otto's cross, only for Scalabrelli to whip it off his head at the vital moment.

Southend's revival, however, was short-lived and the hosts went 2-0 up six minutes into the second half. Massimo Orlando flighted an unbelievable thirty-yard ball to find Tosto in space. His cross was guided home easily by 'Batigol' for his second of the game. On doubling their advantage the home side took their foot off the pedal although Dell'Oglio drew a fine save from Sansome. Fiorentina's substitute goalkeeper Gianmatteo Mareggini produced saves from an Otto shot and a header from Tommy Mooney but was largely untroubled. The home side completed a virtually flawless performance seven minutes from time when another sweeping move allowed Orlando to tap home for an easy third goal.

It is interesting to contrast the two sides' fortunes since this game. Southend have slipped back down to Division Three amid financial struggles. However, worse befell the home side. They duly regained their top-flight place at the end of that one Serie B season and challenged for *La Scudetto* regularly during the late 1990s. The club fell on hard times when the financial mismanagement of President Vittorio Cecci Gori resulted in the selling of heroes like Batistuta and Manuel Rui Costa. The side were relegated but went bankrupt before competing in Serie B. The club folded and a new side, Florentia Viola, emerged, competing in Serie C2, the lowest level of the professional Italian game.

A.C. FIORENTINA 3   **SOUTHEND UNITED 0**
  Batistuta (2), Orlando

A.C. FIORENTINA v. SOUTHEND UNITED

Above: The Aremio Franci Stadium in Florence.

Right: Surely the greatest player to ever face Southend United, Argentinian superstar Gabriel Batistuta.

A.C. Fiorentina: Cristiano Scalabrelli, Mario Faccenda, Vittorio Tosto, Mauro Zironelli, Pasquale Bruno, Lorenzo D'Anna, Antonio Dell'Oglio, Daniele Amerini, Gabriel Batuistuta, Massimo Orlando, Giacomo Banchelli. Subs: Gianmatteo Mareggini (for Scalabrelli), Stefano Pioli (for D'Anna), Gianluca Luppi, Fabio Di Sole and Francesco Flachi (not used)

Southend United: Paul Sansome, Gary Poole, Chris Powell, Keith Jones, Dave Howell, Graham Bressington, Phil Gridelet, Derek Payne, Tommy Mooney, Ricky Otto, Brett Angell. Subs: Jason Lee (for Poole), Jonathan Hunt (for Angell), Simon Royce, Andy Edwards and Pat Scully (not used)

Southend United v. Birmingham City

Rarely could Roots Hall be described as a cauldron of noise, but it was on the day Barry Fry returned to the club he shamelessly abandoned only a few weeks earlier. Fry, who had guided the club superbly during his time, had walked out, taking his backroom staff of Eddie Stein and David Howell with him for the supposedly greener pastures of 'sleeping giant' Birmingham City. Southend fans felt betrayed, with Fry leaving just twenty-four hours after declaring his wholehearted commitment to the Shrimpers.

The build-up to the game was tense, with the police advising Fry to abandon his trademark sortie up the touchline should his side score. They instructed him to stay in the dugout or risk arrest for inciting a riot. Fry, with typical wit, replied, 'I am going need a tin hat for this one ain't I?' Indeed he did – the already simmering tension was brought to boiling point when Stein and Howell needlessly decided to allow their new charges to warm up right in front of the Southend faithful. The matter was not helped by an ill-advised hand gesture towards the crowd by Howell.

Fry emerged from the tunnel at kick-off to a barrage of abuse and hate with raucous chants of 'Judas' engulfing the ground. City's managing director Karen Brady, a prime mover in the heist, was subjected to a torrent of obscene chanting. Southend players knew a victory was needed at all costs and duly delivered despite an even first half.

A major talking point happened in the twentieth minute when referee Paul Danson showed Birmingham striker Andy Saville a red card after appearing to elbow Graham Bressington in the face. The odds were now stacked even further against the visitors but they managed to hold out until the forty-first minute when their resistance was finally broken. The move was a typical Southend goal of the time with a great interchange down the left flank between full-back Chris Powell and winger Ricky Otto. Otto's cross was dangerous and Keith Jones ghosted in to guide the ball past Ian Bennett.

Into the second half and Southend bombarded the visitors' goal and only an inspired performance from Bennett kept the scoreline down. However, the second goal was only a matter of time and it arrived after sixty-six minutes. Fry's former Barnet protégé Jonathan Hunt lashed an unstoppable shot past Ian Bennett who was unable to move before the ball was nestling in the back of his net. The result was put beyond doubt after seventy-five minutes when Gary Poole charged down the right flank and sent over an excellent cross. Lanky striker Jason Lee met the ball superbly and his downward header made it 3-0 to the home side.

The match finished with a bizarre last-minute consolation for Birmingham when the usually reliable Paul Sansome fluffed a clearance and it cannoned into the net off a surprised Paul Peschisolido.

SOUTHEND UNITED 3　　　　　　　　**BIRMINGHAM CITY 1**
K. Jones, Hunt, Lee　　　　　　　　　　Peschisolido

Jonathan Hunt came back to haunt Barry Fry with a great second goal.

SOUTHEND UNITED *v.* BIRMINGHAM CITY

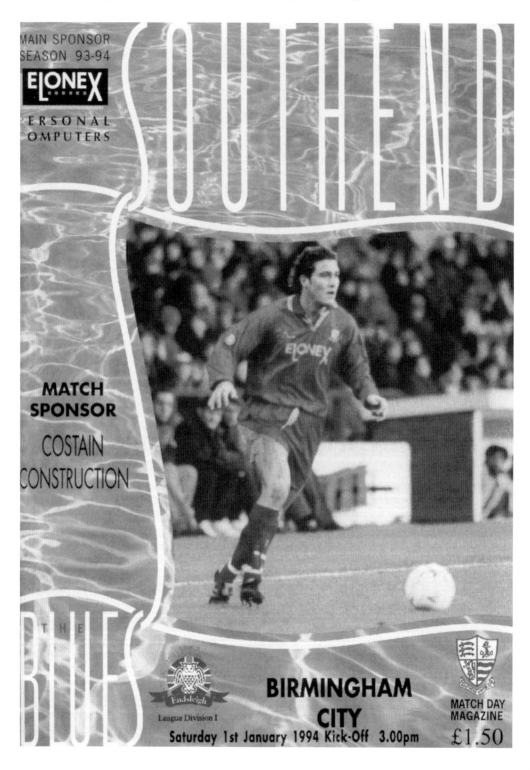

MAIN SPONSOR
SEASON 93-94

ELONEX

PERSONAL
COMPUTERS

MATCH
SPONSOR

COSTAIN
CONSTRUCTION

THE

BLUES

League Division I

**BIRMINGHAM
CITY**

Saturday 1st January 1994 Kick-Off 3.00pm

MATCH DAY
MAGAZINE

£1.50

SOUTHEND UNITED *v.* BIRMINGHAM CITY

Despite the torrent of abuse, Fry was man enough to wait in the tunnel and shake the hand of every Southend player as they left the field. After the match he bemoaned his side's bad luck and cited what he deemed as a harsh sending-off as the turning point of the match.

Barry Fry was sacked as manager of Birmingham City in May 1996 having taken four of the Southend team that played in this game to St Andrews. Poole, Edwards, Otto and Hunt would cost Fry something in the region of £1.5 million in transfer fees. A fifth Southend player, Jason Lee, would later play for Fry again at Peterborough.

Southend United: Paul Sansome, Gary Poole, Chris Powell, Keith Jones, Andy Edwards, Graham Bressington, Jonathan Hunt, Phil Gridelet, Gary Jones, Ricky Otto, Jason Lee. Subs: Derek Payne (for Gridelet), Steve Tilson (for G. Jones) and Simon Royce (not used)

Birmingham City: Ian Bennett, George Parris, Gary Cooper, Dave Barnett, Richard Dryden, Chris Whyte, Ted McMinn, Danny Wallace, Paul Peschisolido, Andy Saville, Kenny Lowe. Subs: David Smith (for Wallace), Roger Willis (for McMinn) and Kevin Miller (not used)

Charlton Athletic v. Southend United

2 April 1994   Football League Division One

An astounding match, which was goal-less at half-time, only to see the home side coast to a three-goal lead within thirteen minutes of the restart.

The first half was fairly even with the only noticeable incident coming just before half-time when Southend's striker, Lee Nogan, on loan from Watford, was crudely tackled by Alan McLeary. Nogan was unable to continue and was replaced by Andy Ansah at half-time. Chances in the first half fell to Charlton's Micky Bennett and Carl Leaburn but were dealt with comfortably by Paul Sansome.

The Valiants took the lead a minute after the restart when the burly front man Leaburn stole a yard on Andy Edwards and crash a shot towards Sansome. He bravely beat out the effort but was helpless to prevent Paul Gorman netting the loose ball.

The home side went further ahead on fifty-five minutes when Leaburn again outmuscled Edwards and powered home an unstoppable header. Three minutes later and Southend looked to be heading for a real hiding when midfielder Alan Pardew picked the ball up from the halfway line and waltzed past several Southend players before slotting the ball home despite a desperate lunge by the luckless Edwards.

However rather than capitulate the visitors rallied and reduced the arrears on sixty-five minutes when the lively Ricky Otto crashed a left-footed drive goalwards. His effort was hacked off the line by Stuart Balmer but Jonathan Hunt was on hand to steer the ball past Mike Salmon.

As the match entered the final five minutes, substitute Andy Ansah took centre stage. On eighty-five minutes Ansah latched onto a long clearance by Mick Bodley and left McLeary and Chapple in his wake before lashing in the corner of the net.

Three minutes later the scores were amazingly level when Southend scored an almost carbon-copy goal. Gridelet this time provided the through ball and Ansah's devastating pace again left the tiring Charlton rearguard floundering. Ansah rounded the 'keeper and slotted home to seal a remarkable comeback. The Blues players and supporters were wild with delight and according to manager Peter Taylor the over-exuberant celebration for the equaliser cost his side the match.

A momentary lapse in concentration undid all their good work and it was a Southend old boy that returned to haunt them. Garry Nelson, discarded by Southend as a youngster but now a wily veteran, had come on as substitute for Gorman after eighty-one minutes and with the clock running down his angled shot was only parried by Sansome. This allowed Pardew to slip in to score a cruel winner in a highly eventful encounter.

CHARLTON ATHLETIC 4   **SOUTHEND UNITED 3**

Gorman, Leaburn, Pardew (2)   Hunt, Ansah (2)

Above left: Ricky Otto was instrumental in a dramatic fightback.

Charlton Athletic: Mike Salmon, Stuart Balmer, Scott Minto, Alan Pardew, Alan McLeary, Phil Chapple, Mark Robson, Micky Bennett, Carl Leaburn, Paul Gorman, Colin Walsh. Subs: Garry Nelson (for Gorman), Peter Garland (for Walsh) and John Vaughan (not used)

Southend United: Paul Sansome, Gary Poole, Chris Powell, Phil Gridelet, Andy Edwards, Mick Bodley, Jonathan Hunt, Derek Payne, Andy Sussex, Ricky Otto, Lee Nogan. Subs: Andy Ansah (for Nogan) Simon Royce and Steve Tilson (not used)

SOUTHEND UNITED V. BOLTON WANDERERS

7 September 1996   Football League Division One

The Shrimpers came into this match still looking for their first win of the season and the form book leant strongly in the favour of their Lancashire visitors, who were unbeaten at the time and would eventually be crowned champions. However, Southend were superb and won every loose ball and chased any lost cause. It could have been so different though, as early as the first minute, when Nathan Blake missed a golden opportunity to give the visitors an early advantage.

It was the home side that opened the scoring on five minutes. A corner was taken by Julian Hails and Keith Dublin flicked on from the near post. Dutch striker Jeroen Boere skilfully hooked the ball into the net, leaving Branagan stranded. Southend had opportunities to increase their lead through John Nielsen and Paul Williams, but conceded a sloppy goal after twenty-three minutes when Alan Thompson's hopelessly miscued shot fell straight to Nathan Blake, who netted the easiest of equalisers.

The Blues stormed back and went ahead two minutes later when the Dane, Nielsen, unleashed an unstoppable twenty-five-yard volley after Williams' shot had been blocked. Mark McNally then tried to emulate Nielsen's effort but Branagan just managed to tip the ball over the crossbar.

Bolton levelled again after thirty-one minutes when Steve McAnespie played a great through ball for the veteran John McGinlay. The wily Scot slipped the ball past Sansome and just out of reach of a despairing lunge from McNally. A memorable first half drew to a close with chances for both sides. Paul Sansome saved well from Blake and a free-kick from skipper Mike Marsh was inches away from finding the corner of the net.

The pulsating action continued with Williams and Blake going close for either side. Bolton's young full-back McAnespie then came to their rescue with two goal-line clearances to deny certain goals from Gridelet and Boere. However, Blues were not to be denied and took the lead for a third time after sixty-five minutes when Boere picked the ball up wide on the right. He cut inside and beat two Bolton defenders before driving the ball past Branagan.

The home side turned the screw on the visitors four minutes later when a hefty clearance from Keith Dublin found Paul Williams in some space. He controlled well and burst past the Bolton rearguard, who were waiting for an offside flag that was not forthcoming. The lithe forward curled the ball around the overworked Branagan and found the corner of the net. Ten minutes from time Southend made it 5-2 when Bolton substitute Andy Todd hacked down John Nielsen in the penalty area and Mike Marsh capped a superb individual display by slotting home the spot kick.

SOUTHEND UNITED 5

Boere (2), Nielsen, Williams,
Marsh (pen)

BOLTON WANDERERS 2

Blake, McGinlay

SOUTHEND UNITED v. BOLTON WANDERERS

 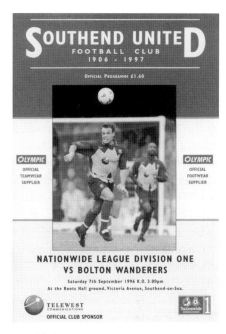

Above left: Man of the Match Mike Marsh inspired the Blues to an unlikely victory.

Southend United: Paul Sansome, Julian Hails, Steve Tilson, Mark McNally, Keith Dublin, Phil Gridelet, Mike
Marsh, Andy Harris, Jeroen Boere, Paul Williams, John Nielsen. Subs: Paul Byrne, Mike Lapper and Leo
Roget (not used)

Bolton Wanderers: Keith Branagan, Steve McAnespie, Jimmy Phillips, Per Frandsen, Gerry Taggart, Chris
Fairclough, Michael Johansen, David Lee, Nathan Blake, John McGinlay, Alan Thompson. Subs: Andy
Todd (for Johansen), Gudni Bergsson (for McAnespie) and Scott Taylor (for Lee)

Plymouth Argyle v. Southend United

24 April 2001   Football League Division Three

This match was a classic Southend United comeback, the visitors having been two goals down after only twenty-three minutes. Home Park had been a happy hunting ground for the Shrimpers, having won on three of their previous four visits to Plymouth.

A pre-match boost came in the return to the starting line-up of midfield maestro Kevin Maher after a bout of 'flu. Ambitiously, manager Dave Webb reverted to a 4-3-3 formation with Tes Bramble, Mark Rawle and his son Danny Webb being the triumvirate in attack. However, Webb's preparations seemed to go straight out of the window when Plymouth took the lead after only seventy-eight seconds. Martin Phillips broke down the right flank and his excellent cross was headed home from eight yards by an unmarked David Friio. The Pilgrims laid siege to Southend's goal with the Frenchman Friio and Ian Stonebridge going close to adding a second.

After nine minutes the talented midfielder Stonebridge latched on to a weak back pass by skipper Phil Whelan and fired in a thunderous shot. Flahavan looked beaten but young defender David McSweeney managed to hack the ball off the goal line. Martin Phillips sent a shot narrowly wide before, on nineteen minutes, home defender Craig Taylor and the Blues' Mark Rawle went in for a fifty-fifty tackle. Both men were injured but Taylor came off worse, being stretchered off with a suspected broken leg. However, Argyle shrugged off the setback and indeed it was substitute Stuart Elliott who created the second goal on twenty-three minutes. His incisive through ball released Michael Evans. He rode Steve Broad's ineffective challenge and easily slotted the ball past the overworked Flahavan.

As the game headed towards half-time Broad received a serious knee injury and was replaced by the veteran Rob Newman. Suddenly, as the fourth official indicated seven minutes of stoppage time, the Shrimpers belatedly sprang into life. Bramble's snap shot was blocked by Larrieu's legs and shortly after his pinpoint cross found Rawle whose header went just past the post. Deep into first-half injury time Blues pulled one back when seventeen-year-old Danny Webb scored his first ever League goal when he steered Rawle's cross into the net from eight yards.

The Southend midfield took a grip on the game in the second half but wasted numerous chances to square the game. Rawle was guilty of considerable profligacy in front of goal, missing a string of decent chances. The forward was then yellow-carded for ungentlemanly conduct after a tussle with David Friio. Southend poured on the pressure and were rewarded in the seventy-second minute when Damon Searle's free-kick from the left flank was inexplicably handled by left-back John Beswetherick. Kevin Maher was coolness personified and netted the spot kick with ease.

As Southend tried for a winner they twice hit the Pilgrims' woodwork in the space of four minutes. On the eighty-minute mark Bramble's shot bounced back off the post with Larrieu well beaten and four minutes later Webb's well-timed strike cannoned back into play.

PLYMOUTH ARGYLE 3   **SOUTHEND UNITED 3**

Friio, Evans, Wotton (pen)   Webb, Maher (pen), Newman

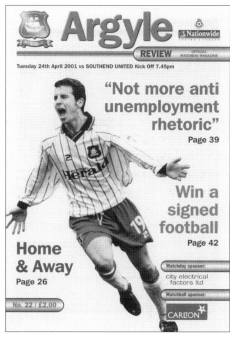

Above left: Rob Newman scored a last-gasp equaliser to seal a dramatic comeback.

For all their effort Blues looked like returning home empty handed when on eighty-seven minutes the home side were awarded a debatable penalty after Newman was adjudged to have handled Phillips' corner. Centre-back Paul Wotton comfortably beat Flahavan from the twelve-yard mark.

The game moved into injury time and the Blues desperately battled for an equaliser and a share of the spoils. Young midfielder Leon Johnson and the luckless Mark Rawle had shots cleared off the line but the team never gave up. Three minutes into injury time the visitors got their just reward when a corner was won on the right side. The industrious Stuart Thurgood fired in a dangerous kick, which allowed Rob Newman to make amends for his earlier aberration by powerfully heading home a well-deserved equaliser.

A titanic struggle ended with a valuable away point gained for the Shrimpers.

Plymouth Argyle: Romain Larrieu, Steve Adams, Jon Beswetherick, David Friio, Paul Wotton, Craig Taylor, Martin Phillips, Wayne O'Sullivan, Ian Stonebridge, Micky Evans, Kevin Wills. Subs: Sean McCarthy (for Stonebridge), Stuart Elliott (for Taylor), Sean Evers, Steve Guinan and John Sheffield (not used)

Southend United: Darryl Flahavan, David McSweeney, Damon Searle, Steve Broad, Leon Johnson, Phil Whelan, Danny Webb, Kevin Maher, Mark Rawle, Stuart Thurgood, Tesfaye Bramble. Subs: Rob Newman (for Broad), Scott Forbes, David Lee, Shane Wardley and Jamie Lunan (not used)

SOUTHEND UNITED *v.* RUSHDEN & DIAMONDS

The Shrimpers had been fielding a fairly new formation in the matches leading up to this Boxing Day clash, with a five-man defence that included player-manager Rob Newman alongside Phil Whelan and Leon Cort. It had served them well at Boothferry Park the previous Friday when a priceless away point was secured against a strong Hull City team in a goal-less draw. The only team change was to bring in Barrington Belgrave for Mark Rawle in attack. However, the defensive tactic fell apart in the first half against Football League newcomers, Rushden & Diamonds, when their giant Jamaican centre forward Onandi Lowe terrorised the Southend rearguard.

The visitors took the lead after just five minutes when pacy winger Paul Hall harried left-back Damon Searle into a weak header across his own area. The loose ball fell invitingly into the path of midfielder Garry Butterworth, who beat Flahavan with a well-executed half-volley. From the restart the Shrimpers should have equalised but Carl Hutchings failed to connect to a Thurgood centre. Diamonds promptly broke upfield and former Southend youngster Ritchie Hanlon thundered a twenty-five-yard shot narrowly over the crossbar.

Southend created several more chances to draw level but found visiting 'keeper Billy Turley in great form. The former Leyton Orient custodian denied Carl Hutchings twice before Diamonds increased their lead. With thirty-five minutes on the clock, Lowe burst clear from Newman and Cort and sent a hopeful ball across the penalty area. The ball should have been cleared by Whelan, who instead completely missed his kick, allowing Scott Partridge to side foot past an unprotected Flahavan.

Facing a two-goal deficit Newman substituted himself and brought on pacy winger Steve Clark, making his second appearance on loan from West Ham United. This resulted in a move back to a conventional 4-4-2 formation as Southend pressed unsuccessfully for a goal before half-time.

Southend attacked the South Stand goal in the second half and pressurised the visitors with a succession of corners after the restart. After fifty minutes a Kevin Maher corner kick saw Carl Hutchings' close-range shot parried by Turley, only for Leon Cort to drive in the rebound for his first goal in League football. Buoyed by the breakthrough, a lapse in concentration saw the Blues nearly concede again after superb work from Lowe resulted in a great chance for Hanlon. Luckily Flahavan expertly blocked the midfielder's shot with his legs to deny him. The Blues levelled on fifty-nine minutes when another swift attack saw a deft pass from Tes Bramble release Barrington Belgrave. The former Norwich, Plymouth and Yeovil striker had time to select his shot and duly dispatched the ball into the bottom left-hand corner past a despairing dive from Turley.

SOUTHEND UNITED 4

Cort, Belgrave (2), Bramble

RUSHDEN & DIAMONDS 2

Butterworth, Partridge

SOUTHEND UNITED v. RUSHDEN & DIAMONDS

Above left: Leon Cort's first senior goal put the Blues on the road to an amazing comeback.

Chances came thick and fast and Southend took the lead on sixty-seven minutes when a brilliant through ball by Belgrave released Bramble for a one-on-one with the advancing 'keeper. Bramble just beat Turley to the ball and his shot trickled towards an unguarded net. Despite an effort by Underwood to get back and clear, the ball carried on rolling goal-bound before coming to a rest just inches over the line. The Blues then had Darryl Flahavan to thank for denying a Diamonds equaliser when he saved a point-blank header from Onandi Lowe. Southend secured the points in a pulsating match when Belgrave mesmerised the Diamonds' defence before a swift one-two with Bramble resulted in Belgrave's second of the match.

Having been booed off at half-time, the Blues had completed a remarkable comeback to secure their first League 'double' of the campaign, having beaten Rushden 1-0 at Nene Park earlier in the season. A scintillating display of attacking football in the second half saw the majority of a 5,878 Boxing Day crowd go home very happy indeed.

Southend United: Darryl Flahavan, Steve Broad, Damon Searle, Rob Newman, Phil Whelan, Leon Cort, Stuart Thurgood, Kevin Maher, Tesfaye Bramble, Barrington Belgrave, Carl Hutchings. Subs: Steve Clark (for Newman), Mark Rawle (for Bramble), Leon Johnson (for Hutchings) Danny Kerrigan and Danny Gay (not used)

Rushden & Diamonds: Billy Turley, Adam Sanbrook, Paul Underwood, Garry Butterworth, Mark Peters, Jim Rodwell, Paul Hall, Ritchie Hanlon, Onandi Lowe, Andy Burgess, Scott Partridge. Subs: Duane Darby (for Rodwell), Gary Setchell (for Partridge), Mike McElhatton (for Butterworth), Gary Mills and Tony Pennock (not used)

Southend United v. Queens Park Rangers

LDV Vans Trophy Area Semi-Final

Rarely in recent times have the Shrimpers been more of an underdog in a home game. The visitors to Roots Hall, Queens Park Rangers, were riding high in Division Two, hot on the heels of league leaders Plymouth Argyle. Their team was full of well-known names: Paul Furlong, Kevin Gallen and Marc Bircham to name a few. The Shrimpers were slumped at the wrong end of Division Three and an LDV Vans Trophy Area final looked a distant dream. However, the West Londoners were torn apart by a rampant Blues team.

Southend started brightly when Jamie Stuart's free-kick was sliced by Danny Shittu and a thunderous drive from skipper Kevin Maher brought a fine save out of Chris Day in the Rangers' goal. The opening goal came on twelve minutes when a low Mark Gower cross was well controlled by top scorer Leon Constantine, who then drilled an unstoppable left-footed shot into the corner of the net. A chance of a Rangers equaliser went begging just two minutes later when Clarke Carlisle shot weakly straight at Darryl Flahavan following a decent cross from Terrell Forbes on the right flank. Drewe Broughton could have extended the Blues' advantage but blazed high and wide following good work from a short corner contrived between Jay Smith and Mark Gower. Southend's single-goal lead remained intact at half-time.

The second half began cagily and Rangers should have drawn level when Furlong was put clean through by Martin Rowlands; however, Flahavan sped out to block bravely at his feet. The Blues astonishingly went 2-0 up in the sixty-seventh minute when a Rangers corner was cleared to Gower. His deft pass put Steve Clark in the clear and the inconsistent winger bore down on the visitors' goal. Danny Shittu attempted to crudely upend the former West Ham youngster but Clark held his balance and steered the ball past a stranded Day. Two minutes later the match was effectively over when the Shrimpers scored again. The magical Mark Gower burst clear on the left wing and his pinpoint cross was met by Drewe Broughton. His looping header dipped in sweetly under the crossbar, despite a valiant attempt from Carlisle to clear his lines. Minutes later Constantine capitalised on another mistake by the ponderous Shittu and his shot narrowly missed the post of Day's goal. Rangers almost pulled one back when Gallen blazed wide following a neat build-up between Furlong and substitute Eric Sabin.

Blues continued to attack and Broughton nearly netted in the seventy-eighth minute following a fine through ball from Jay Smith, but Day successfully turned his firm shot around the post. From the resultant corner Leon Cort's powerful header was well parried by the overworked Rangers custodian, but Broughton was on hand to tap the rebound into the net for an incredible 4-0 scoreline.

Rangers were beaten and bloodied, and despite a spectacular injury time save by Flahavan from Gino Padula's free-kick, the visitors offered scant evidence of their renowned attacking prowess.

SOUTHEND UNITED 4   **QUEENS PARK RANGERS 0**

Constantine, Clark,
Broughton (2)

SOUTHEND UNITED v. QUEENS PARK RANGERS

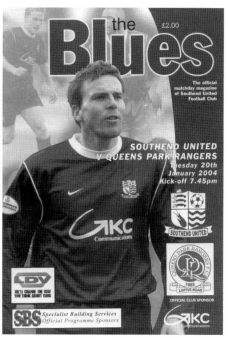

Above: Leon Constantine scored Southend's first goal in this match.

Southend's caretaker manager, Steve Tilson, was delighted with his team's annihilation of supposedly superior opposition. His counterpart, Ian Holloway, described the match as the most humbling experience of his career. Blues earned an Area final clash with bitter Essex rivals Colchester United and an eventual Millennium Stadium appearance against Northern Area winners Blackpool.

Southend United: Darryl Flahavan, Duncan Jupp, Jamie Stuart, Leon Cort, Mark Warren, Jay Smith, Mark Gower, Kevin Maher, Leon Constantine, Drewe Broughton, Steven Clark. Subs: Che Wilson (for Stuart), Michael Kightly (for Clark), Neil Jenkins (for Gower), David McSweeney and Carl Emberson (not used)

Queens Park Rangers: Chris Day, Terrell Forbes, Gino Padula, Danny Shittu, Clarke Carlisle, Matthew Rose, Marc Bircham, Martin Rowlands, Dean Marney, Kevin Gallen, Paul Furlong. Subs: Eric Sabin (for Marney), Steve Palmer (for Bircham), Dennis Oli (for Gallen), Nicky Culkin (not used)

Other titles published by Tempus

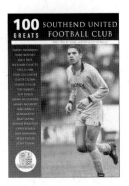

Southend United Football Club 100 Greats
PETER MILES & DAVE GOODY

This book pays tribute to 100 of the greatest players in Southend United's history, including goalscorers like Harold Halse and Brett Angell, goalkeepers like Ted Hankey, and club stalwarts like Alan Moody and Billy Best. Comprising biographies, illustrations and statistical information, this compilation by Peter Miles and Dave Goody celebrates the careers of these players and makes a superb record of their achievements for the club.
0 7524 2177 8

Southend United Football Club
PETER MILES & DAVE GOODY

With nearly 200 illustrations, including action shots, team photographs, player portraits, programme covers and cartoons, this book illustrates the fascinating history of Southend United Football Club since its formation in 1906. Many rare and previously unpublished images document the highs and lows, from the Southern League Second Division to Football League Division One. This is an essential read for all fans of the club.
0 7524 2089 5

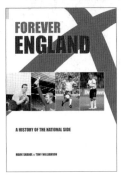

Forever England A History of the National Side
MARK SHAOUL & TONY WILLIAMSON

This insightful and fascinating account, which covers the careers of England's all-time great players and the team's successes, failures and near misses, is an essential read for anyone interested in the history of the three lions. From the amateur gentlemen of the 1870s to the stars of the early twenty-first century, with many wonderfully evocative illustrations, it is the definitive history of England's national football team.
0 7524 2939 6

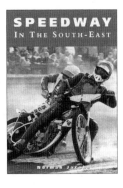

Speedway in the South-East
NORMAN JACOBS

The south-east of England has been one of the great centres of Speedway over the years, and it is still home to some of Britain's leading teams. This book covers the history of those tracks and promotions and the exploits of some of the riders that have starred. Written by speedway enthusiast Norman Jacobs and featuring many rare photographs, this book is a must for anyone with an interest in the sport.
0 7524 2725 3

If you are interested in purchasing other books published by Tempus, or in case you have difficulty finding any Tempus books in your local bookshop, you can also place orders directly through our website

www.tempus-publishing.com